OF MIND AND OTHER MATTERS

Of Mind and Other Matters

NELSON GOODMAN

HARVARD UNIVERSITY PRESS

Cambridge, Massachusetts, and London, England

This book is printed on acid-free paper, and its binding materials
have been chosen for strength and durability.

Library of Congress Cataloging in Publication Data

Goodman, Nelson.
  Of mind and other matters.

  Includes index.
  1. Philosophy—Addresses, essays, lectures.
I. Title.
B29.G619 1984   191   83-12868
ISBN 0-674-63125-0 (alk. paper) (cloth)
ISBN 0-674-63126-9 (paper)

To

Kinky
Snubby
Tweedledee
Randy
Angie
Debby
Susan
Trushka

for help and hindrance

Preface

For the reader familiar with my work, this book brings up to date the discussion of many topics studied in my other books, but it also explores some new subjects. For the reader unfamiliar with my work, it provides through examples and sidelights an idea of the nature and major themes of my thinking. For both readers, it may convey a sense of the unity of a course of thought that ranges over fields from science policy to dance criticism, from literary theory to cognitive psychology, from language to the function of museums, and from education to the making of worlds.

Moreover, I hope it may help to dissociate my views from others often mistaken for them. I am a relativist who nevertheless maintains that there is a distinction between right and wrong theories, interpretations, and works of art; I believe neither that a literary work is determined by the intent of the author nor that all interpretations are equally right; I am a nominalist who lets anything be taken as an individual, and a rather behavioristically oriented cognitivist who recognizes the cognitive functions of emotion. I am an anti-realist and an anti-idealist—hence an irrealist. I oppose both the scientism and the humanism that set the sciences and the arts in opposition to each other. And I am a theorist concerned with practice as informing and informed by theory.

Much of the material in this book has been incorporated in papers published during the past ten years in a wide variety of periodicals and collections; but some sections are entirely new and others, in the interest of continuity, clarity, or correctness, have undergone rearrangement, augmentation, abridgment, and sometimes important revision. Partly because my work has tended to cut across traditional boundaries, the chapter headings do not sort the several discussions according to sharply segregated topics; some sections could have equally well been put in a different chapter. There is some repetition of arguments and examples, but I hope their recurrence in varied contexts may be more illuminating than irritating.

I am grateful to Catherine Elgin for valiant help in organizing the book and improving its content, to Joseph Ullian for permission to include material from a paper we collaborated on, and to the various editors and publishers responsible for the original appearances of many of the papers (see "Sources and Acknowledgments").

Nelson Goodman

Harvard University

Contents

OF MIND AND OTHER MATTERS

Abbreviations for books by Nelson Goodman

SA *The Structure of Appearance,* third edition (1977) D. Reidel
    Publishing Co. (first published 1951).

FFF *Fact, Fiction, and Forecast,* fourth edition (1983) Harvard
     University Press (first published 1954).

LA *Languages of Art,* second edition, third printing (1976) Hackett
    Publishing Co. (first published 1968).

PP *Problems and Projects,* Hackett Publishing Co., 1972.

WW *Ways of Worldmaking,* second printing (1981) Hackett
    Publishing Co. (first published 1978).

I. Thought

*T*his chapter examines and undertakes to reform some current notions concerning cognition and its role in science, art, and perception. Beginning with the keynote remarks for an international symposium on science policy, it goes on to discuss visual comprehension and aesthetic experience. It proceeds to consider the implications of recent clinical studies of the ways different brain damages affect different cognitive skills. And it concludes with an attack on the old issue of the status of mental images, arguing that talk of 'pictures in the mind' need involve no commitment for or against the existence of any mind or any pictures in it.

All told, the chapter illustrates my conception of epistemology as the philosophy of the understanding and thus as embracing the philosophy of science and the philosophy of art.

1. SCIENCE AND SIN

At a meeting of the Council, manywhere and oft upon a time, the Chief of State announced the agenda as follows: "Today we must discuss ways of dealing with the gravest current threats to our country: invasion, inflation, crime in the streets, the plague, and science."

Science has long been associated with evil. Science, after all, was the first sin. The Garden of Eden was lost for partaking of the fruit of the tree of knowledge of good and evil, lost not for

lust but for curiosity, not for sex but for science. Science is missing from the list of the seven deadly sins only because it has the
more exalted status of Original Sin. Folklore is shot through with
such maxims as "Curiosity killed the cat", and "What you don't
know won't hurt you". Even the old saying "A little knowledge is
a dangerous thing" does not tell us whether more knowledge is
more dangerous or less so, and leaves the impression that the
best and safest state is total ignorance.

The view of science as evil explains such time-honored policies with respect to scientists and their work as "Out with their
tongues" or "Off with their heads"; "Burn the books"; "Hide
what is known and block inquiry". Policies of this sort were
adopted by rulers who felt that a ruler should know more than
those who are ruled. That idea, though admirable enough in itself, could be realized in either of two ways: by the rulers becoming learned or by the subjects being kept ignorant, and the
latter course often seemed the more feasible.

More fundamentally, policies of suppression were perpet-
uated by an almost universal fear of the unknown. What lies behind the closed door may be a murderous monster or an unbear-
able truth. And the secret our enemy knows may enable him to
destroy or dominate us. Keep the door closed, then, and block
the way to anything not already known.

Fear of the unknown extends to the arts as well. Totalitarian
regimes often ruthlessly suppress all artistic innovation; book
burning has a parallel in the destruction of works and exhibitions of avant-garde paintings and sculpture. Thus, perversely,
the arts are recognized along with the sciences as powerful ways
of knowing and of remaking our worlds.

Nevertheless, such policies of suppression are always being
undermined by the irresistible fascination of the mysterious and
occult. Not only do we want for ourselves the secrets we fear
when others have them, but sheer curiosity is even more universal and compelling than lust, and the mischances that may result
are less easily thwarted or aborted. The heart of an idea may
begin to beat at the moment of conception.

Science is indeed unsafe. Neither our curiosity nor the dangers it may lead us into have determinable limits. Yet no way is known for preventing the exercise of curiosity. Full protection would require a painstaking study of the creative processes, of the faculties of discovery, and the invention of ways to inactivate them. But that would amount to scientific investigation; and if science is a sin, then seeking thus to eradicate it would involve committing it.

Yet dangerous as science may be, and despite that dead cat mentioned in the proverb, I doubt if the dinosaur or any other species ever became extinct as a result of excessive curiosity. And without science, we ourselves might well be extinct by now from typhoid and tuberculosis or rats, from bacteria or viruses or insects or powerful predators. That might, of course, be taken as an argument for the suppression of science; for if, from lack of curiosity, we become extinct, then we shall be perpetually safe.

This may suggest a policy of encouraging benign and discouraging malignant science: support the search for cures of disease but prohibit the search for new means of destruction. But how can that be managed? Discovery of a way to cure or prevent a malady is also almost inevitably discovery of a way to propagate it. Science has already given physicians the weapons they could, if they liked, use to decimate mankind. Not the findings of science but the ways these are used can be classified into the good and the evil.

In recent times, science has both gained something and lost something through a change in the moral atmosphere. On the one hand, the association of science with other sins is no longer damaging in an age when lust and some of the others have been transformed, in the popular mind, from cardinal sins into cardinal virtues. On the other hand, rather than being carried along with other former sins to a position of veneration, science is now commonly contrasted with them and condemned for being inimical to all these properly 'human' propensities. Science is looked upon as destructive of every human interest and feeling, as displacing wants and satisfactions and values with cold calculations, as mechanizing and congealing life itself, rather than as an expression of one of our most essential and rewarding drives.

3

So far I have been talking of science policy as policy formulated and implemented by a government or a society and, moreover, as policy imposed upon scientists for the prevention or restraint or advancement—that is, the control—of science. But science policy may also be formulated and administered by scientists for the improvement of method, the coordination of the several sciences and of varied programs of research, for the training of investigators and the development of the facilities and conditions for carrying their work forward. And each of *us* needs a policy to guide us in deciding the quantity and quality of attention and of support or opposition we should devote to science, what we should expect from it, and how wary we should be of it. Our policy might lead us at one extreme to a vote for or contribution toward a basic research center, or at the other to a demand that advanced mathematics be dropped from a curriculum.

The trouble is that science policies, whether established by government, by religion, by society, by scientists, or by laymen, are too often based upon the fear and fascination of the unknown, or upon a distaste for or mistrust of the intellectual, or directed toward the acquisition or preservation of power, too often distorted by adulation of science as the only path to insight and discovery, or by confusion of science with uses and misuses of its results.

Science is no monster come lately to devour us but a manifestation of our profound need to explore, to explain, to inquire—not for the sake of controlling nature, defeating our enemies, or improving our comforts but simply for the sake of discovering, of knowing, of understanding. Once a discovery is made, knowledge acquired, an explanation achieved, science passes on to examine what is still not understood. How the results it leaves behind are to be employed is less a scientific than a technological and administrative question that must be dealt with in full recognition that the results of science are never final or complete, and that danger lies rather in what we don't know than in what we do.

But science is not the only way of advancing knowledge.

Practice, perception, and the several arts are equally ways of gaining insight and understanding. The naive notion that science seeks truth, while art seeks beauty, is wrong on many counts. Science seeks relevant, significant, illuminating principles, often setting aside trivial or overcomplicated truths in favor of powerful unifying approximations. And art, like science, provides a grasp of new affinities and contrasts, cuts across worn categories to yield new organizations, new visions of the worlds we live in.

On the other hand, science is no enemy of the arts. Misguided advocates of the humanities often feel they must counter the pernicious influence of the sciences. Science becomes associated with unfeeling intellect, the humanities with pure emotion, thus slandering both. Intellectual effort is motivated by profound need and provides deep satisfaction; and the emotions often function also as cognitive instruments. Neither art nor science could flourish if it did not give satisfaction, or if satisfaction were the only aim. Constable urged that painting is a science, and I suggest that science is a humanity. Putting them in opposition misconceives and hurts both.

Policy for science needs to be based on a sound awareness of what science is and is not, of how far it can be distinguished from technology, and of its relationship to philosophy, the arts, and all other ways of knowing.

2. LOVE AND UNDERSTANDING

The art historian James Ackerman, in a recent paper, often shows an understanding of my work uncommon among writers who are not professional philosophers. For example, while even philosophers have often fumbled the notion of exemplification, Ackerman not only sees and accepts the main point but provides a pertinent illustration of his own.[1]

His main worry is that I do not sufficiently stress the role of the viewer—the audience—in art, and that I therefore underrate the subjectivity of art and the drastic difference, on this score,

1. See note 3 of his "Worldmaking and Practical Criticism", *Journal of Aesthetics and Art Criticism* 39 (1981) 249–254.

between art and science. He writes that science unlike art is primarily a matter of experimentation and proof; that in art unlike science the observer cannot be counted on to act consistently, and concludes:

I cannot accept the concept of autonomous aesthetic objects. The aesthetic experience can occur only when an observer is on hand to have it; it is compounded not only of emanations from the object but also of the mode of receptivity of the observer. The event differs a little or a lot for different observers.

Our disagreement, I think, is less about the nature of art than about the nature of science. Whereas Ackerman looks upon science as "concerned primarily with the processes of experimentation and proof", I think of it, in the words of Lewis Thomas, as

a mobile unsteady structure . . . with all the bits always moving about, fitting together in different ways, adding new bits to themselves with flourishes of adornment as though consulting a mirror, giving the whole arrangement something like the unpredictability and unreliability of living flesh. . . . The endeavor is not, as is sometimes thought, a way of building a solid, indestructible body of immutable truth, fact laid precisely upon fact. . . . Science is not like this at all.[2]

Despite Ackerman's early remark concerning *Ways of Worldmaking* that

Insofar as it deals with art, it struck me as standing in relation to classical aesthetics as relativity theory does to classical physics,

he seems sometimes to forget that my rejection of the usual contrasting of the scientific-objective-cognitive with the artistic-subjective-emotive depends as much on the artificiality of fact as on the factuality of aesthetic rightness, and as much on the variety and dynamics of worldmaking and the pervasive role of the worldmaker as upon the difference of right from wrong in the arts. I do not deny that our experience of art is highly variable but rather insist that so also is our experience of everything else. I do not hold that there are 'autonomous aesthetic objects' but rather deny that there are any 'autonomous objects' at all. I do

2. *Harvard Magazine* 83 (1980) 19–20.

not suppose that judgments of art can be established by proof from observational premises certified by confrontation with a fixed and found world, but neither do I suppose that any other judgments can be so established.

Standards of rightness in science do not rest on uniformity and constancy of particular judgments. Inductive validity, fairness of sample, relevance of categorization, all of them essential elements in judging the correctness of observations and theories, do depend upon conformity with practice—but upon a tenuous conformity hard won by give-and-take adjustment involving extensive revision of both observations and theories. Standards of rightness in the arts are likewise arrived at, tentatively and imperfectly, on the basis of but also amending a ragged practice. Our ways of seeing may test and be tested against a way shown in a painting.

My insistence on the cognitive aspect of art makes Ackerman and others fear that I am bent on anaesthetizing the aesthetic. What I want to emphasize is that pleasure or even ecstasy alone, without insight or inquiry, without recognition of significant distinctions and relationships, without effect on the way we see and understand a world including the object itself, can hardly be considered aesthetic. And I am sure that Ackerman does not regard as aesthetic the pleasure derived from family albums and centerfolds.

No doubt he is urging rather that the cognitive aspect alone, understanding without love, is not enough. Here I must first point out that, even granting that emotion is required for aesthetic experience, the emotion surely need not be love. Boredom, distaste, disgust aroused by bad works of art are no less aesthetic; and revulsion, depression, horror, and hate are more prominently and appropriately involved than love in our experience of some great tragic dramas and paintings of bloody martyrdoms.

Emotions and feelings are, I agree, required for aesthetic experience; but they are not separable from or in addition to the cognitive aspect of that experience. They are among the primary means of making the discriminations and the connections that

7

enter into an understanding of art. Emotion and feeling, I must repeat once more, function cognitively in aesthetic and in much other experience. We do not discern stylistic affinities and differences, for example, by 'rational analysis' but by sensations, perceptions, feelings, emotions, sharpened in practice like the eye of a gemologist or the fingers of an inspector of machined parts. Far from wanting to desensitize aesthetic experience, I want to sensitize cognition. In art—and I think in science too—emotion and cognition are interdependent: feeling without understanding is blind, and understanding without feeling is empty.

Most of what Stefan Morawski says[3] on the cognitive aspects of the aesthetic seems to me right. The different ways that works may function cognitively do need to be studied and compared; and my tentative development and application of a taxonomy of symbols, symbol systems, and types of symbolic relations was intended to be a step in that direction. I also agree that cognition is involved not merely in understanding works themselves but in understanding the several worlds—of perception, science, practice—that we make and live in; and this is a major theme of *Ways of Worldmaking.*

But I take exception to some of Morawski's remarks along the way. For instance, he writes that in the case of "any great specimen of geometrical abstraction" (e.g., a work by Klee or Kandinsky) "the response is primarily hedonistic. Granted, cognition is implied by impressions that build relevant patterns which are more or less adequate to the inner structure of the works. Yet the main attention is focused by an arousal of pleasant feelings." To some extent, pleasant feelings of varied sorts may, as means for discerning the rightness or novelty of the patterns, contribute to understanding of the works; but to take the feelings as ends in themselves is to put aesthetic experience in the same category as a hot bath, and is somewhat like rating Einstein's theory by the emotional satisfaction it yields. (See further *LA*, pp. 243–244.) Again, when Morawski writes of works of abstract expression-

3. In "Three Observations on *Languages of Art*", *Erkenntnis* 12 (1978) 119–128.

ism that their "chief impact is emotional due to the dynamic expression of colors, lines, shapes", and later that "language is a better means to embody the cognitive message than are colors, sounds, gestures", he is taking the notion of the cognitive much more narrowly than I do. For me, cognition is not limited to language or verbal thought but employs imagination, sensation, perception, emotion, in the complex process of aesthetic understanding.

In his discussion of cultural relativism, Morawski argues for a 'nature-culture tension'. Like many others, perhaps most, he is reluctant to forego a single reality or fixed forms of the understanding, holding that the way the world is and the characteristics of the human being put constraints on the variety of right world-versions and upon languages. I have stated the case for radical relativism before, but here I mention only two points. (1) The argument from 'linguistic universals' seems to me utterly without force since whatever significant structural features may be designated as such universals, a language lacking such features can be invented, learned, and used. The modified claim that languages that can be acquired as *first* languages must have certain characteristics is vague and suspect of question-begging until "language" is more explicitly defined and the characteristics in question specified. (2) Ontological relativism does not imply that all world-versions are right but only that at least some irreconcilable versions are right. Examples abound, and a single world can hardly answer to conflicting versions.

3. KNOWING THROUGH SEEING

In *Languages of Art* (I,3) I attacked James J. Gibson's contention that realism of representation can be measured in terms of geometrical optics by how nearly the bundle of light rays delivered from a picture duplicates a bundle delivered from what is represented. He has now abandoned that contention.[4]

Furthermore, we agree in rejecting criteria of realism based on the deceptiveness of pictures or on their similarity to their sub-

4. See "The Information Available in Pictures", *Leonardo* 4 (1971) 10–19.

jects. And I am more in agreement with him than he seems to realize in insisting upon a significant distinction between paragraphs and pictures—between linguistic and pictorial symbols. Although I wrote that we must *read* a picture—in other words, interpret rather than merely register it—an appreciable part of my book is devoted to defining the distinctions between linguistic, pictorial, and other symbol systems; and I entirely agree that there is no vocabulary of picturing as there is of saying.

Still, our meeting of minds is not complete. In the first place, I do not agree that reverse perspective cannot be consistently applied. A long opaque rectangular box, viewed obliquely, may be drawn in standard perspective as in Figure 1 (a) or in reverse perspective as in Figure 1 (b). Drawings of the box viewed from the end will be as in Figure 2. If the box is transparent, then Figure 2 (b) will serve as a drawing in standard perspective (with the outer square for the near end) or in reverse perspective (with the inner square for the near end).

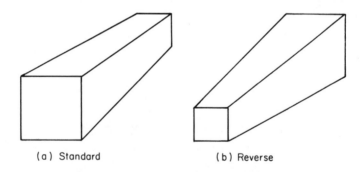

(a) Standard   (b) Reverse

Figure 1.

In the second place, I am wary of Gibson's proposal for a new theory of realistic representation. His outline is somewhat vacillating and vague. In what he calls a formal definition, he says that the optic array from a picture provides information of the *same kind* as does an optic array from the object, but a few sentences later he requires, more reasonably, that the *same information* be provided. Again, he says that optical information "consists of in-

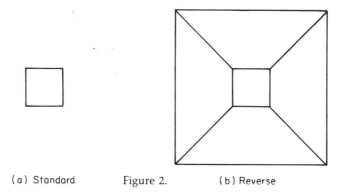

(a) Standard   Figure 2.   (b) Reverse

variants, in the mathematical sense, of the structure of an optic array", but he does not specify, mathematically or otherwise, what these relevant structural invariants are. Later he seems to identify these invariants with the "invariant distinctive features of objects". But this seems to complete a circle: in saying that the information provided by optic arrays consists of the invariant distinctive features of the object represented, are we saying anything more than that what is constant among the several views or pictures of an object is the object they represent—a statement that may be true enough but that is notably lacking in information.

If these difficulties are resolved by a fuller statement of the theory, I have other worries. Is it not clear that the same information about the opaque box is provided by Figure 1 (b), as a drawing in reverse perspective, and by Figure 1 (a), as a drawing in standard perspective; and that more information about the box is provided by Figure 2 (b), as a drawing in reverse perspective, than by Figure 2 (a), as a drawing in standard perspective? Moreover, the information yielded by these drawings obviously depends not only upon them but also upon the system according to which they are interpreted. And this points to my most serious misgiving about Gibson's proposal: that the notion of 'the information provided by an optic array' is much too elliptical to serve the purpose at hand. The amount and kind of information derived from an optic array or anything else is usually no constant function of what is encountered but varies with the processing. A symbol may inform in as many different ways as there are contexts and systems of interpretation.

Marx Wartofsky probes into some fundamental and far-reaching philosophical problems illustrated by questions about perspective.[5] What he writes is in general accord with my own views as set forth not only in my published works but in papers that were not available to him when he was working on his.

On several minor points, I differ with him somewhat. In the first place, he seems to suppose that the usual realistic picture represents its subject very much as a mirror does, and writes: "Thus Brunelleschi's injunction to 'draw it the way it looks in the mirror' is the craftsman's practical version of incorporating the laws of geometrical optics with the rules of pictorial representation." What this overlooks is that my mirror image, quite unlike me or my realistically painted or photographic portrait, *writes with the left hand.* If a camera were made or a painter induced to produce pictures with the orientation of the mirror image, would such pictures then be more faithful? Wartofsky's argument would be strengthened not weakened had he noticed this point.

Second, I think he has not given sufficient attention to the drastic change in Gibson's position on perspective between his discussions before and after publication of *Languages of Art,* or to the criticisms I have made of Gibson's newer theory.

Third, I take exception to his description of perception as "rule-following". Granted that our perceiving and our picturing may be influenced by talk, "rule-following" is far too limited a term for what Wartofsky is discussing here. Even linguistic behavior and comprehension, it seems to me, are only rarely directed by formulated rules; and the notion of an unformulated rule escapes me. Our seeing and our painting, moreover, are primarily nonverbal, and may be more drastically modified by confrontation with an El Greco or a Braque than by any string of words.

5. In "Rules and Representation: The Virtues of Constancy and Fidelity Put in Perspective", *Erkenntnis* 12 (1978) 17–36.

Early in his paper, Wartofsky seems to be contending that a physicalistic account of what is seen can be faithful, correct, basic, while a phenomenalistic one cannot: that we actually *see* the circular shape of the table top and learn to notice the momentary elliptical appearance, rather than see the elliptical appearance and learn to infer the constant circular physical shape. Later, though, he makes it clear that any claim that either version is more correct than the other is suspect, and that the question of absolute epistemological priority—of *what* account describes pure visual experience unadulterated by interpretation or inference—is empty.

Of course, as is evident all the way from *The Structure of Appearance* through *Ways of Worldmaking*, I heartily agree. Most subjects in a psychological experiment where two spots are flashed in quick succession a short distance apart report seeing one spot moving from the first position to the second. Some, however, report seeing two successive flashes. Now are they actually seeing differently or are they seeing the one moving spot, as we see the elliptical shape, but reporting they see the two flashes as we report we see the circular shape? Short of specifying the vocabulary, phenomenalistic or physicalistic, to be used in giving the report—and that would beg the question—we cannot find out. The question what they were seeing actually or natively or purely or without interpretation, etc. is vacuous.

But now Wartofsky is confronted by a hard question. If neither of the two types of description nor any other is exclusively faithful or correct, if none is more right or fundamental than another, then what if anything distinguishes correct from incorrect description? As Wartofsky puts it: "Between the Scylla of historical relativism and mere descriptivism (in which each norm is its own warrant of 'correctness' . . .) and the Charybdis of essentialism, there is a narrow strait which I hope to navigate." If his seamanship at best avoids the shoals without actually reaching port, the seas are indeed heavy in these waters.[6]

Mere relativization is not enough. Under different frames of

6. As I have noticed in the final chapter of *WW*.

reference, the earth moves and the earth stands still. We are tempted to say that the facts are determined when the framework is chosen; but then we must recognize that facts and frameworks differ only in scope, and that a mistake may be made in either. An astonomer miscalculating the position of a planet very likely has a wrong fact under a right framework, while a guard who shot prisoners ordered to stand still, explaining that they then moved rapidly around the sun, seems to have a right fact under a wrong framework. Yet the guard's framework and the astronomer's may be the same.

I am convinced, with Wartofsky, that there is no one correct way of describing or picturing or perceiving 'the world', but rather that there are many equally right but conflicting ways—and thus, in effect, many actual worlds. We must, then, inquire into the standards, compatible with such multiplicity, of rightness of renderings of all sorts, in all media, in symbol systems of every variety. This strikes me as one of the most pressing problems of present-day philosophy, and one of the most perplexing. All the same, I am not sure that we are much further from understanding the criteria for rightness of rendering in general than we are from understanding the special case that we call truth.

4. ON RECONCEIVING COGNITION

Some important trends in epistemology are illustrated in recent papers by Howard Gardner[7] and Marx Wartofsky.[8]

Gardner has had the audacity to intrude consideration of the anatomy and operations of the brain into a philosophical symposium on a book (*Languages of Art*) written by an author not notably inclined to physicalism, materialism, or behaviorism. Shouldn't I then unfurl the philosopher's moldy banner that reads: "No inference to epistemology from physiology"? Shouldn't I remind Gardner that tracing nerve impulses from re-

7. "A Psychological Investigation of Nelson Goodman's Theory of Symbols", *The Monist* 58 (1974) 319–326.

8. "Art, Action and Ambiguity", same, pp. 327–338.

ceptors to parts of the brain does not help at all in explaining consciousness, and protest that loss of a skill when a certain component of the brain is damaged tells us no more about the nature of that skill than the fact that loss of an eye causes blindness tells us about vision?

I think Gardner would justly reply that such objections completely misrepresent what he is trying to do. When we discover that one of two apparently very similar skills is lost or impaired under a given type of brain damage while the other survives intact, we are forced to look for a significant correlative difference between the two skills. Cases in point are that of a man whose facility with words is lost while his facility with numerals is preserved, and of a man whose ability to read English vanishes while his ability to read music remains. Again, if two seemingly very disparate skills are both impaired when a particular part of the brain is injured, we must look for a significant affinity between them. The damage may affect both skills through being in the intersection of the two correlated regions or paths in the brain. Our whole conception of the nature of and interrelations among various cognitive processes, our whole analysis and taxonomy of psychological functions, is called to account by such cases. Conversely, a well-conceived theory of skills points to questions to be asked of, and interpretations to be given to, anatomical and neurological data. Indeed, the relationship of such clinical research as Gardner describes to psychology and epistemology is so plain that all these disciplines may well be thought of as aspects of a single science of cognition. This, I think, is the reason why Gardner as a psychologist is now working with brain surgeons in a hospital and why we as philosophers must be concerned with what he and they are doing.

Reflection upon such work brings out a contrast between two different routes of inquiry that relate the mind and the brain. Let me call them *universalism* and *differentialism.* The first is manifest in the work of one contemporary school of linguistics and psycholinguistics. Natural languages are examined for features common to all; and such features are then conjectured to be necessary characteristics of any language that could be acquired as a first language. The ground for these universal characteristics or constraints is sought in structural properties of the mind that might in turn point to neurological or brain structures or mechanisms accounting for such linguistic universals. Universalism of this sort may be questioned on many grounds: (1) Any collection of languages (or anything else), however heterogeneous, will have some common features; and the claim that the common features actually found are necessary in all first-learnable languages is a gratuitous one immune to feasible experimental test. (2) The linguistic universals usually cited, such as subject-predicate form, seem to be features of translations into our language rather than of the languages translated. That all languages (or at least all languages we can understand) are translatable into a language that we understand and that has certain features is at worst question-begging and at best a dubious basis for ascribing such features to those languages. Finally, (3) brain and nerve mechanisms that would plausibly correlate with universals of the kind in question are difficult to imagine or to seek.

Sharply contrasting with universalism is what I call *differentialism*. Here the various linguistic and nonlinguistic symbol systems that must be processed in the exercise of various skills are distinguished from and related to one another according to what promise to be significant features. The resultant partial and tentative systematization of skills both is tested by and puts to test the observations made in the clinic and the laboratory. The serviceability of the theoretical framework may be corroborated or challenged by the data; and the data may sometimes be given illuminating reinterpretation in the light of the theory. One looks not for universal characteristics but for significant differences—and then looks for anatomical and neural correlates. No claim is made that the distinguishing features noted are the only—or the only important—ones or that symbol systems of certain kinds could not be learned as first systems. But some of the differences among symbol systems—for example, that between 'digital' linguistic and 'analog' nonlinguistic systems—are such that the differences in type of mechanism appropriate for processing systems of these differing kinds are readily envisaged and sought.

Both Wartofsky and Gardner are concerned with the interplay in cognition between habit and problem-solving. Wartofsky stresses situations where our familiar procedures are confronted by an ambiguity (or a vagueness or an obscurity or a multiplicity of function)[9] that calls for deliberation, decision, reorientation and reorganization—situations where habitual responses and established routines are challenged by something novel and puzzling. These situations he finds to be the 'moments of truth' in art. Obviously they are equally crucial in science and in life in general. Without the ability to master and to modify habits we should be lost. Understanding consists largely of the interdependent skills of establishing and of breaking habits as may be required.

Although Gardner started from the standard conjecture that, in general, the left half of the brain processes linguistic or differentiated or digital symbol systems, while the right half processes pictorial or continuous or analog systems, he found evidence that the left hemisphere characteristically deals with what has become familiar, mastered, learned, recognized, while the right half characteristically deals with the novel, with what has yet to be categorized, codified, organized. This suggests that Wartofsky's dichotomy between the ability to learn, to establish effective habits or routines, and the ability to unlearn, to reorganize, to deal with ambiguities and obscurities, to solve problems, may be correlated with the division of the brain into left and right hemispheres. But Gardner points out that this need not result in abandoning the initial hypothesis; for the material embodied in language or other linguistic systems has already undergone considerable processing, considerable organization and codification. Thus, having been linguistically en-

---

9. Wartofsky uses the term "ambiguity" very loosely and broadly—not in the narrower technical sense that distinguishes ambiguity from unclarity, complexity, subtlety, and other departures from the easy and obvious.

coded involves having become familiar, and the two hypotheses tend to merge.

A second look raises some doubts about this. For one thing, I am uncomfortable about any assumption such as is implicit here that one particular type of symbol system is more native than or is somehow epistemologically prior to another. Again, I should hardly expect that a novel problem couched in a familiar linguistic system (say a complicated new problem in arithmetic) would be handled by the right hemisphere, or that a nonlinguistic skill such as billiard playing or style discrimination in painting would be transferred to the left hemisphere when well mastered.

Perhaps, though, the two hypotheses are related in another—and more intimate—way. In working with even a very familiar typically nonlinguistic dense[10] symbol scheme we are incessantly confronted with what is not quite familiar. Nothing is fixed completely and finally here; no identification is ever fully determinate. On the other hand, in working with a familiar typically linguistic articulate scheme, we find even the most novel situation presented in terms of a familiar alphabet—a set of a few well-known atomic characters. Along these lines may lie the best hope of illuminating the alliance of the novel and the nonlinguistic with the right hemisphere, and the alliance of the familiar and the linguistic with the left.

Still, much more study is needed. Some difficult questions remain, as Gardner recognizes, in determining the nature and locus of the familiarity involved in the various experimental findings. Wartofsky's interesting distinction between categorial and non-categorial ambiguity is far from enough. Consider the several varieties of unfamiliarity that are illustrated when a person who reads English only is confronted with

(1) a passage printed in French
(2) a passage printed in Greek
(3) a passage in German script
(4) an inverted picture
(5) a blurred picture.

10. For an explanation of my use of the technical terms in this passage see *LA*, IV.

In the first case, the letters but not the words are familiar; in the second, not even the letters; and in the third, not even the articulation into letters. The fourth and fifth cases, where neither words nor letters are involved, give trouble of two other kinds. In novelty, no novelty itself, are many novelties.

Aspects of a general conception of cognition are reflected in the emphasis in both papers upon habituation and problem-solving. Wartofsky and Gardner participate in the current transition from static absolutism to dynamic relativism in epistemology. The search is no longer for a raw given or fixed forms of the understanding or a unique and mandatory system of categories. Rather, knowing is conceived as developing concepts and patterns, as establishing habits, and as revising or replacing the concepts and altering or breaking the habits in the face of new problems, needs, or insights. Reconception, reorganization, invention, are seen to be as important in all kinds of knowing as they are in the arts.

This may also explain to some extent why, in a symposium on symbols and skills in the arts, I have said very little that pertains primarily or exclusively to the arts. I am inclined to think that many of the currently crucial problems in aesthetics are problems in the general theory of knowledge, and that many of the traditional concepts and questions of aesthetics, along with our habit of thinking of the arts in isolation from other matters, are obsolescent. In short, I think we have in the field of aesthetics a prime example of Wartofsky's syndrome for a 'categorial' problem-solving situation, where the need is not for answers to ready-made questions but basic reconsideration and reorganization.

5. CAN THOUGHTS BE QUOTED?

Some questions raised by Paul Hernadi about quotation[11] lead quickly to tough problems about the nature of thought.

A direct quotation must contain a replica of what is quoted,

11. In "More Questions Concerning Quotation", *Journal of Aesthetics and Art Criticism* 39 (1981) 271-280.

either spoken or written, or of a translation thereof. The words

> Juanita said, "He's caught"

directly quote what Juanita said even though they are written in English and she spoke in Spanish.

But what if Juanita did not speak or write of her conquest but only thought of it? Do the words

> Juanita thought, "He's caught"

directly quote her thought? That may seem an innocent and easy question; but when Hernadi first raised it in conversation with me, and wondered if the answer would be positive on the ground that thoughts are in words, I began to worry.

The conviction that thoughts are always in words has thrived on the recent philosophical focus on language, but has been primarily sustained by the incredibility of or incomprehensibility of the most familiar alternatives: looking upon the mind as a sort of motion-picture theater, or upon thoughts as ideas couched neither in words nor pictures nor any other symbols.

Yet the view of thinking as purely verbal leaves many an open question. What of the difference we do perceive, and describe however inadequately as between "having and not having a picture in the mind" of a person or place? What happens when we "have a thought we cannot put into words"? Furthermore, since we do work and communicate overtly with symbols of all kinds, can thinking be with words alone? And do we have in the mind images of words but no images of anything else? Or if a thought of a word is not an image, what is it?

To such questions, I can respond only with some tentative and conditional guesses or counterquestions: (1) We can obviously think *of* pictures, but can we think *in* pictures?—Yes, if we can think *in* words. (2) Are there thoughts without words?— Yes, if there are thoughts without pictures. (3) Are there pictures in the mind?—Yes, if there are words in mind. (4) How can a picture be in the mind?—Well, how can a word be in the mind?

All this doesn't answer Hernadi's question, but may attest to its significance. Does

> Juanita thought, "He's caught"

directly quote her thought? Hmm. . . .

6. ON THOUGHTS WITHOUT WORDS

Thought about laws of form[12] ought, perhaps, to include consideration of some troublesome questions about the form of thought. Indeed I have argued in *Ways of Worldmaking* and elsewhere that the forms and the laws in our worlds do not lie there ready-made to be discovered but are imposed by world-versions we contrive—in the sciences, the arts, perception, and everyday practice. How the earth moves, whether a world is composed of particles or waves of phenomena, are matters determined not by passive observation but by painstaking fabrication. Species do not come prepackaged, separated by unbridgable gaps or inexorable dictates of nature, but depend upon the relative weight we put upon certain features for given scientific purposes. The issue between uniformitarianism and catastrophism—over whether or not a cataclysm breaks a law of nature—is a question not of whether nature is lawful but of what generalizations we formulate and dignify as laws.[13] The arts and sciences are no more mirrors held up to nature than nature is a mirror held up to the arts and sciences. And the reflections are many and diverse.

I do not want to argue that thesis further here; and I am not by any means suggesting that the *forms thought of* are the *forms of thought*. I shall be concerned rather with questions about the forms of thought itself—questions that strike me as no less pressing, and sometimes rather more slippery, than questions about the form of objects, appearances, biological species, sociological groups, or mathematical concepts.

Many psychologists and analytic philosophers look upon thinking as entirely verbal, upon thoughts as always in words. This tendency has been strengthened by recent focusing of attention upon linguistics, but may be sustained primarily by the incredibility of the alternative notion of thoughts as disembodied images floating in the mind. Yet on closer examination the verbal view, despite its virtues, raises some troublesome questions.

12. The allusion is to the title "Laws of Form" of the conference where this paper was first delivered; see "Sources and Acknowledgments" below.
13. See my "Uniformity and Simplicity" in *PP*, pp. 347–354.

Whether or not all thoughts are in words, some surely are. We can think of all sorts of things—of tables, idiots, and Saturn's rings, of ships and cabbages, and kings—and of words. Words differ from the rest of these in that we can think *in* words but not *in* cabbages (at least in anything like the same sense). What is it, though, to think *in* words? Is a thought of a cabbage just a thought of a word for (and as for) a cabbage? That won't work; for then a thought of a word involves thought of a word for a word, and so on back ad infinitum. Thinking *in* cannot be reduced to thinking *of*. Words we think in are somehow 'in the mind', while the cabbages or words we think of are not. But what can this mean? What sort of thing is a mind that words can be in and how can words be in it?

The difference between what we think *in* and what we think *of* seems something like the difference between what we speak in and what we speak of. We can speak *in* words or *in* English without speaking *of* words or *of* English, and we can speak of cabbages but not in cabbages. A notable difference between the *of* and the *in* here is that speaking *of* cabbages or *of* words does not require producing them. This suggests that thinking not only is like but may actually *be* speaking, that silent thought is in words we speak to ourselves. Such a proposal has the virtue of not needing a mind for words to be in. Rather, thinking like speaking is performance.

Best known for a theory of this sort is John B. Watson, who held that all silent thought is 'subvocal speech', explained as bodily activities—especially of the laryngeal system—that approximate those of overt speech but fall short of producing an utterance. Now since speech consists of producing utterances, and utterances must be uttered, 'subvocal speech' is not speech at all. The nature of unspoken speech, or of an unuttered utterance is somewhat paradoxical, and we might even jest that what we usually regard as a theory of thought as verbal actually treats all covert thought as thought without words. But of course the paradox is rather easily resolved if we recognize that having words in mind or thinking silently in words no more implies that we have anything called a mind or words in it than having peace as a hope implies that we have anything called peace or a hope. "Word" and "mind" in such contexts function syncategoremati-cally as nondenotative fragments of phrases that, under Wat-son's theory, denote bodily activities or states.

All this is quite in keeping with Watson's aim of making thought accessible, at least in principle, to scientific observation. He holds that not only ostensibly verbal thinking but all covert thinking whatsoever is subvocal speech. Although he mentions 'nonlanguage forms of thought' in one place, he is there merely emphasizing that such nonlaryngeal covert behavior as writing, drawing, gesturing, and tracing with the eyes or fingers may be included under 'language activity and other activity substitutable for language activity'. He writes:

The term "verbal" here must be made broad enough to cover processes substitutable for verbal activity, such as the shrug of the shoulder and the lifting of the brow ... Thinking then might become our general term to cover all subvocal behavior.[14]

He is not by any means countenancing thought in pictures or images. This view of thought as exclusively verbal has been so widely accepted that any talk of pictures in the mind has become rather disreputable.

Ironically, when we make sense as we have of unspoken speech or inaudible utterances, we open the way to making like sense of undrawn pictures or invisible images. How can there be pictures in the mind? Well, how can there be words in the mind? Just as "having words in the mind" applies to certain activities of the organism without presumption of a mind or words in it, so "having pictures in the mind" applies to certain other activi-ties—submanual drawing or painting, or subvisual seeing—without presumption of a mind or pictures in it. Just as some thoughts are in inaudible words, so others are in invisible pic-tures. Pictures in the mind and thoughts in pictures are no more and no less mythical than words in the mind and thoughts in words—a conclusion likely to shock those who pride themselves on the scientific probity of insisting that all thought is verbal.

14. *Psychology*, 2nd ed. (Philadelphia: J. B. Lippincott Co., 1924), p. 346.

Yet while most of us are much more practiced in speaking than in picture-making—much better at uttering or writing words we have in mind than at drawing or painting or carving images we have in mind—pictures are in general no less clear in our minds than are words. For this reason and others I think the loose formula that thinking in words or pictures involves activities approximating those of actually producing such words or pictures needs some modification.

First, a thought may involve not, or not only, activities on the way toward but rather, or also, the state of readiness for production. Second, and more important, thinking in words or pictures may often involve preparing or being ready not, or not only, to produce such words or pictures but rather, or also, to judge a word or picture produced or presented as agreeing or not agreeing with the one in mind. When I succeed in calling up a mental picture' of a place I saw briefly long ago, my ability to produce a picture may be negligible but I am much readier than before to accept some pictures as right and reject others as wrong, and to suggest changes. And there may be various stages of readiness along the way: before I have fully in mind the word or picture I want, I may be able to reject one after another as not the right one. In such cases, where in effect the word or picture or other symbol is only circumscribed within certain classes, the thought is a vague or general notion.

The judgments called for in varied contexts may be on varied grounds. When a thought both in and of a word is in question, an utterance or inscription may be rejected as not a replica[15] (or 'token') of that word. When a thought is not of words but of cabbages, a word may be rejected rather as not referring to cabbages, an object may be rejected as referred to not by "cabbage" but by "king", and a picture may be rejected either as not of a cabbage or as not the picture or sort of picture required.

Just here lies the difference between thought of a word for cabbages and thought of that word also *as for* cabbages; that is, the difference between thought of a word for cabbages and

---

15. On the technical use of "replica" see *SA*, pp. 262–264.

thought of cabbages. When judgment of presented utterances or inscriptions is according to how they are spelled, whether they are in English, whether they have seven letters, the thought is of a word that though a word for cabbages is not of that word *as for* cabbages. The thought is of the word as for cabbages only if the judgments are on the ground of what the word denotes. What is involved in verbal thought of the fictitious, such as centaurs, is slightly more complex: that a centaur-word—for instance "centaur" itself—be produced or prepared for and that such compounds of that word as "centaur-description" and "centaur-picture" be judged by what they denote, and that presented descriptions and pictures be judged by whether they are denoted by the appropriate compounds.[16]

Even with the modification outlined, however, "preparation for producing or judging" is still rather too narrow a formula, reflecting an obsolete view of *perception* as a purely passive process. Not since the advent of modern cognitive psychology has such a view been defensible. What and even whether we perceive depends heavily on our state of perceptual readiness.[17] Habit, context, explicit instruction, interests, and suggestions of all kinds can blind or activate our perception, conceal or reveal a mountain or a molehill. Far from merely recording what is before us, perception participates in making what we perceive; and for perception there are processes and stages of preparation. Thinking in words or pictures or other symbols may involve not only preparation for producing or judging but also for perceiving— seeing, hearing, etc.—such symbols.

While all the preparation and preparedness, and even the differences between judging by different criteria, are here construed in terms of activities and states of the organism, no reduction of the mental to the physical is implied. For in the first place, I think a dichotomy of things into the mental and the physical is no more tenable than a dichotomy into those made of energy and

16. See further *PP*, pp. 221–240, and *LA*, pp. 21–26; also Israel Scheffler's *Beyond the Letter* (London: Routledge & Kegan Paul, 1979), pp. 29–36.
17. See Jerome S. Bruner "On Perceptual Readiness" in *Psychological Review* 64 (1957) 123–152.

those made of matter. "Physical" and "mental" apply more aptly to functions of an organism that itself belongs under neither term or both. In the second place, and more important, I have not said that these activities and states of the organism *constitute* thought, but only that they are *involved in* thought. I take no stand here on the question whether anything more, such as conscious-ness, is also required for thought. I am concerned rather with what distinguishes thought in words from thought in pictures and thought in symbols of other kinds. I am concerned less with the nature of thought than with its modes, less with its substance than with its forms.

We saw how the proposed way of looking at the forms of thought avoids trouble about unspoken speech and unwritten writing, and dismisses the cinema-in-the-head as a chimera. It accommodates thought in pictures, gestures, diagrams, and other symbols as easily as thought in words, and accommodates thoughts of the fictive as well as thoughts of the factual. Thoughts may be specific or general according as we are pre-pared to judge a presented symbol severely or leniently. And some familiar phenomena otherwise awkward to account for máy be explained: for example, having a 'naked' idea, couched in no word or picture or other symbol, may occur when the process of making ready for the appropriate production of judgment of a symbol is at an early stage; for the paths of preparation for sym-bols of different kinds may coincide for a time, and only diverge and become specialized later.

Moreover, we can now deal more circumstantially with Paul Hernadi's troublesome question (see I,5 above) concerning the quotation of thoughts. Does the statement

Juanita thought, "He's caught"

directly quote Juanita's thought? Yes, if Juanita thought in those words, but not otherwise; for a direct quotation must contain a replica of what is quoted. But the answer is rather more compli-cated than that. We have seen that what we call 'thought in words' need strictly involve no perception or production of words in or out of the mind but only activities or states of preparation for such perception or production. Thus, even though in the latter oblique sense Juanita may be said to have 'thought in words', there can be no verbal replica and so no actual direct verbal quotation of her thought. However, in much like the oblique sense that we say her thought is in words, we may say it can be directly quoted in words: the quotation will contain replicas of the words for whose production or perception her thought involved preparation.[18]

Earlier, I stressed the distinctions between what we think *of* and what we think *in:* a cabbage we think *of* is not composed of letters, while the word "cabbage" that we think *in* does not smell. The forms of what we think of are not in general the forms of what we think in. But obviously, a third factor now needs to be taken into account. Since thought is in symbols, we might slip into supposing that the forms of thought are to be found exclusively in the symbols thought in, forgetting that thinking in words or pictures or other symbols is not, strictly, using words or pictures or any symbols at all, but is a process of preparation or state of preparedness for producing or judging or perceiving such symbols. The forms of these processes and states must surely enter into consideration of forms of thought and be distinguished from the forms of what we think in and what we think of. When we think of an object in symbols, the object but not the thought or the symbols in question may happen to be square, the symbols but not the object or the thought verbal, the thought but not the object or the symbol fleeting.[19]

Nevertheless, while the three sorts of forms are distinct, they are surely not independent of each other. The forms of processes and states pertaining to readiness to produce or judge or perceive a symbol are in many respects determined by the syntactic and semantic form of the systems that the symbols to be produced or

18. On the general question of the relation between pictures 'in the mind' and what is pictured, the reader will find much of interest in Robert Schwartz's "Imagery", *Proceedings of the Philosophy of Science Association* 2 (1980) 285–301.

19. For an interesting commentary on the above discussion by Daniel Dennett, see "Why we think about what we do about why we think about what we do", *Cognition* 12 (1982) 219–227.

judged or perceived belong to; for instance, thinking in characters of a notational system involves activities and states differing in form from those that thinking in ordinary language or in pictures involves. And the forms of what we think of are by no means independent of the forms of what we think in. The form of classical music heard is affected and constrained by the structure of the notation in which the score is written. And I maintain that a world, much like a musical performance, is the creature of and is informed by a version constructed in a symbol system. But I promised not to argue that thesis here.

What I do urge is that the study of laws of form must include—and will find an intriguing field of exploration in—the study of how the processes and states involved in thought are related, dynamically and statically, to each other, of how they affect and are affected by the symbols to be produced or perceived or judged, and of how the forms of the symbol systems we think in and employ in our world-versions determine the forms of the worlds we think about and live in.

II. Things

The first chapter considered operations of understanding; the second asks after what there is. But since in my view what there is consists of what we make, the two topics are intimately related. Sometimes I characterize the lines of thought sketched here as *irrealism*. Irrealism does not hold that everything or even anything is irreal, but sees the world melting into versions and versions making worlds, finds ontology evanescent, and inquires into what makes a version right and a world well-built.

The first three sections examine questions often raised about *Ways of Worldmaking*. How can we make worlds that existed before us? With no ready-made world as a touchstone, how can there be criteria of truth and rightness? How may some conflicting statements both be true? How can the recognition of many actual worlds be reconciled with the rejection of all merely possible worlds?

The final section concerns nominalism, sometimes thought to be incompatible, or at least uncomfortable, with my irrealistic relativism. Why should such a relativism not be as open to platonistic as to nominalistic world-versions? Since for the thoroughgoing irrealist everything including individuals is an artefact, why does he not find classes of classes of classes, for example, as admissible as individuals? All these questions are grounded in a misunderstanding of my brand of nominalism. Once that is corrected, they answer themselves; for the irrealist insists upon distinguishing between well-made and ill-made (or unmade) worlds, and the nominalist's proscription is against a way of making. Irrealism and nominalism are independent but entirely compatible. Indeed, nominalism neither conflicts with nor implies nor is implied by my other philosophical views.

1. NOTES ON THE WELL-MADE WORLD

Since it seems obvious that words are usually different from what they refer to, that we cannot in general make anything by merely describing or picturing it, and that not all descriptions or pictures are right, how can I talk of worldmaking, find facts fluid, acknowledge conflicting truths, and suggest that the distinction between world and version is elusive? Here I want to review and clarify some themes of *Ways of Worldmaking*, discuss some common objections to it, and reaffirm some of its paradoxes.

Monism, Pluralism, Nihilism

Some truths conflict. The earth stands still, revolves about the sun, and runs many another course all at the same time. Yet nothing moves while at rest. We flinch at recognition of conflicting truths; for since all statements follow from a contradiction, acceptance of a statement and its negate erases the difference between truth and falsity.

Usually we seek refuge in simple-minded relativization: according to a geocentric system the earth stands still, while according to a heliocentric system it moves. But there is no solid comfort here. Merely that a given version says something does not make what it says true; after all, some versions say the earth is flat or that it rests on the back of a tortoise. That the earth is at rest according to one system and moves according to another says nothing about how the earth behaves but only something about what these versions say. What must be added is that these versions are true. But then the contradiction reappears, and our escape is blocked.

Should we rather consider "The earth is at rest" and "The

earth moves" as incomplete fragments of statements, true or false only when completed in some such way as in "The earth moves relative to the sun" or "The earth is at rest relative to Mount Everest"? This does not work either; for what can these statements mean? Perhaps, in the former case, "If the sun is at rest, then the earth moves". But then the antecedent and consequent are themselves fragments of statements, without truth-value until completed; and so on ad infinitum. Or should we translate to "If the sun's position is plotted as a point, the earth's positions will be plotted as a path"? Then, since the diagrams are simply (nonverbal) versions, we are back to simple-minded relativization.

How, then, are we to accommodate conflicting truths without sacrificing the difference between truth and falsity? Perhaps by treating these versions as true in different worlds. Versions not applying in the same world no longer conflict; contradiction is avoided by segregation. A true version is true in some worlds, a false version in none. Thus the multiple worlds of conflicting true versions are actual worlds, not the merely possible worlds or nonworlds of false versions.

So if there is any actual world, there are many. For there are conflicting true versions and they cannot be true in the same world. If the notion of a multiplicity of actual worlds is odd and unpalatable, we nevertheless seem forced to it by the intolerable alternative of a world in which contradictory and therefore all versions are true.

But where are these many actual worlds? How are they related to one another? Are there many earths all going along different routes at the same time and risking collision? Of course not; in any world there is only one Earth; and the several worlds are not distributed in any space-time. Space-time is an ordering within a world; the space-times of different worlds are not embraced within some greater space-time. Worlds are distinguished by the conflict or irreconcilability of their versions; and any ordering among them is other than spatio-temporal.

Yet however intricately and plausibly this idea may be developed, how can there really be many worlds? There may be many stars, many planets, many chairs, many things, many events; and truths about them may conflict and contrast in all sorts of ways. But "world" is all-inclusive, covers all there is. A world is a totality; there can be no multiplicity of totalities, no more than one all-inclusive whole. By assigning conflicting versions to different worlds, we preclude composition of these totalities into one. Whatever we may mean by saying that the motion of the Earth, or of different earths, differs in different worlds, we rule out any more comprehensive whole comprised of these. For a totality cannot be partial; a world cannot be a piece of something bigger.

So if there is any world, there are many, and if many, none. And if none, what becomes of truth and the relationship of a version to what it describes? Parmenides ran into this trouble long ago: because truths conflict, we cannot describe the world. Even when he said "It is" he went too far. "It is" gives way to "They are"; and "They are" to "None is". Monism, pluralism, nihilism coalesce.

Part of the trouble comes, as in the Kantian antinomies, from stretching some terms or notions beyond their reach. So long as we keep within a version, "world" or "totality" is clear enough, but when we consider conflicting true versions and their several worlds, paradox enters. This sometimes leads to utter resignation, sometimes to an irresponsible relativism that takes all statements as equally true. Neither attitude is very productive. More serviceable is a policy common in daily life and impressively endorsed by modern science: namely, judicious vacillation. After all, we shift point of view and frame of reference for motion frequently from sun to earth to train to plane, and so on. The physicist flits back and forth between a world of waves and a world of particles as suits his purpose. We usually think and work within one world-version at a time—hence Hilary Putnam's term "internal realism"[1]—but we shift from one to another often. When we undertake to relate different versions, we introduce multiple worlds. When that becomes awkward, we drop the worlds for

1. See, for example, his *Meaning and the Moral Sciences* (London: Routledge and Kegan Paul, 1978), pp. 123–140.

the time being and consider only the versions. We are monists, pluralists, or nihilists not quite as the wind blows but as befits the context.

According to one variety of solipsism, only I exist but this holds for each of the many people in the world. Somewhat analogously, one might say that there is only one world but this holds for each of the many worlds. In both cases the equivocation is stark—yet perhaps negotiable.

Ontology Evanescent

Or have we gone too far too fast? May the conflicts we encounter among truths turn out on closer examination to amount less to genuine differences in what is said than to differences in manner of saying? Rather than disagreements on objective fact, are these merely superficial differences, chargeable to the varying perspectives and languages of our versions, with the real world to be sought beneath such surface disturbances?

Consider again, for example, the true statements that the earth is at rest, that it revolves around the sun, that it dances a jig, and so on. The suggestion is that the conflicts between these have no more to do with the earth, sun, or other heavenly bodies than do the different orders in which these objects may be described, but arise from the differing biases of the several versions; and that statements concerning the direction, speed, and acceleration of motion are different ways of describing the neutral facts of variation in distance between objects at different times. If all features responsible for disagreements among versions are thus dismissed as artificial, truths will no longer conflict in a way that calls for different worlds.

But once we recognize that some supposed features of the world derive from—are made and imposed by—versions, 'the world' rapidly evaporates. For there is no version-independent feature, no true version compatible with all true versions. Our so-called neutral version of motion is as prejudiced as any other; for if direction and speed and acceleration are relative to observer and frame of reference, so also is distance between objects. And, as I shall argue below, the objects themselves and the time and space they occupy are version-dependent. No organization into units is unique or mandatory, nor is there any feature-less raw material underlying different organizations. Any raw stuff is as much the creature of a version as is what is made out of that stuff.

Yet if all features of a world are creatures of a version, are generated and imposed by the version, what can they be imposed upon? The question is pertinent but slightly awry. The world of a true version is a construct; the features are not conferred upon something independent of the version but combined with one another to make the world of that version. The world is not the version itself; the version may have features—such as being in English or consisting of words—that its world does not. But the world depends upon the version.

Some inkling of what I mean by saying we make worlds may begin to glimmer here: we make versions, and true versions make worlds. This calls for further explanation on more than one score. How can we be said to make worlds by making versions, when making a true description of a chair, for example, falls far short of making a chair? And while we make versions, and we hope some true versions, we can hardly make versions true. Moreover, if there is no independent world to match a version against, what constitutes truth and what are the tests for it?

How to Make Things with Words[2]

That we can make the stars dance, as Galileo and Bruno made the earth move and the sun stop, not by physical force but by verbal invention, is plain enough. That we by like means also make things what they are in respects other than motion has now begun to be clear. From here a short step leads to the conclusion that we make the things themselves. But that, on the face of it, seems silly. Downright refutations are ready at hand in the form of challenges to produce forthwith, by means of a potent descrip-

2. With apologies to J. L. Austin, who did not explicitly include making things in what we do with words.

tion, an extra planet, a chair to sit in, or a tender beefsteak. Inevitable failure is taken to prove the point.

But I have not said that we can make a steak or a chair or a world at will and as we like by making a version. Only if true does description make things; and making a true version can be hard work. But isn't that begging the question? Doesn't that amount to saying that versions can make only what is already there? And how can that properly be said to be making at all? If versions can make neither what is nor what is not already there, that seems a closed case against their making anything at all.

Yet I am not ready to give up; 'being already there' needs further examination, and finding what is already there may turn out to be very much a matter of making.

I sit in a cluttered waiting room, unaware of any stereo system. Gradually I make out two speakers built into the bookcase, a receiver and turntable in a corner cabinet, and a remote control switch on the mantel. I find a system that was already there. But see what this finding involves: distinguishing the several components from the surroundings, categorizing them by function, and uniting them into a single whole. A good deal of making, with complex conceptual equipment, has gone into finding what is already there. Another visitor, fresh from a lifetime in the deepest jungle, will not find, because he has not the means of making, any stereo system in that room. Nor will he find books there; but in the books and plants I find he may find fuel and food that I do not. Not only does he not know that the stereo set is one; he does not recognize as a thing at all that which I know to be a stereo system—that is, he does not make out or make any such object.

Now you may complain that all I am doing is applying a different term to a familiar process to bring out the constructive aspect of cognition. And you may ask, as Israel Scheffler has, how we can reasonably say that we, or versions, make the stars, which existed long before us and all versions.[3] Let me defer that question for a moment to look at a slightly different case.

Has a constellation been there as long as the stars that com-

3. See his "The Wonderful Worlds of Goodman", *Synthese* 45 (1980) 201–209, and my reply, pp. 211–215.

pose it, or did it come into being only when selected and designated? In the latter case, the constellation was created by a version. And what could be meant by saying that the constellation was always there, before any version? Does this mean that all configurations of stars whatever are always constellations whether or not picked out and designated as such? I suggest that to say that all configurations are constellations is in effect to say that none are: that a constellation becomes such only through being chosen from among all configurations, much as a class becomes a kind[4] only through being distinguished, according to some principle, from other classes.

Now as we thus make constellations by picking out and putting together certain stars rather than others, so we make stars by drawing certain boundaries rather than others. Nothing dictates whether the skies shall be marked off into constellations or other objects. We have to make what we find, be it the Great Dipper, Sirius, food, fuel, or a stereo system.[5]

Still, if stars like constellations are made by versions, how can the stars have been there eons before all versions? Plainly, through being made by a version that puts the stars much earlier than itself in its own space-time. As the physicist J. A. Wheeler writes:

The universe does not exist "out there" independent of us. We are inescapably involved in bringing about that which appears to be happening. We are not only observers. We are participators . . . in making [the] past as well as the present and the future.[6]

Truthmaking

Yet our making by means of versions is subject to severe constraints; and if nothing stands apart from all versions, what can

4. That is, a *relevant*—sometimes miscalled *natural*—kind.
5. And this, as I have mentioned earlier, goes all the way down. Not all differences between true versions can be thought of as differences in grouping or marking off within something common to all. For there are no absolute elements, no space-time or other stuff common to all, no entity that is under all guises or under none.
6. In *Science 81* (June) p. 67.

be the basis and nature of these constraints? How can a version be wrong about a world it makes? We must obviously look for truth not in the relation of a version to something outside that it refers to but in characteristics of the version itself and its relationships to other versions. Could a version perhaps be false somewhat in the way a jigsaw puzzle can be wrongly put together, or a motor fail to run, a poster to attract attention, or a camouflage to conceal?

When the world is lost and correspondence along with it, the first thought is usually coherence. But the answer cannot lie in coherence alone; for a false or otherwise wrong version can hold together as well as a right one. Nor do we have any self-evident truths, absolute axioms, unlimited warranties, to serve as touchstones in distinguishing right from among coherent versions; other considerations must enter into that choice. Let us begin by looking at some of these that have to do with varieties of rightness other than truth.

Validity of inductive inference, though a property of a relation among statements, requires truth neither of premises nor of conclusion; a valid inductive argument may even yield a false conclusion from true premises. What, then, is required for inductive validity? Certain formal relationships among the sentences in question *plus* what I shall call right categorization. Now a category or system of categories—a way of sorting—is not sentential, is not true or false; but use of wrong categories will make an induction invalid no matter how true the conclusion. For example, if an emerald is said to be grue just in case it is either examined before a given time and determined to be green or is not so examined and is blue, then the same formal rules that lead from evidence statements about green emeralds to the hypothesis "All emeralds are green" will also lead from evidence-statements about "grue emeralds" to the hypothesis "All emeralds are grue"; but the former inference is valid, the latter not. For although the evidence-statements are true in both cases, and the truth of both hypotheses is as yet undetermined, "grue" picks out a category wrong in this context, a nonrelevant kind. Valid induction runs within—is constrained by—right categories; and only through distinguishing right categories from among classes in general can we distinguish valid from invalid induction. But what makes a category right? Very briefly, and oversimply, its adoption in inductive practice, its entrenchment, resulting from inertia modified by invention.[7] Why some categories rather than others have become entrenched—a subject of avid philosophical debate—does not matter here; the entrenchment, however achieved, provides the required distinction. Rightness of categorization, in my view, derives from rather than underlies entrenchment.

Inductive validity is not only an example of rightness other than truth but is also one of the criteria applied in the search for truth: a hypothesis validly inferred is favored over an alternative invalidly inferred from the same evidence. Yet how is acceptability as determined by such considerations related to truth, and does this help us answer the question what constitutes truth? Obviously we cannot equate truth with acceptability; for we take truth to be constant while acceptability is transient. Even what is maximally acceptable at one moment may become inacceptable later. But *ultimate* acceptability—acceptability that is not subsequently lost—is of course as steadfast as truth. Such ultimate acceptability, although we may seldom if ever know when or whether it has been or will be achieved, serves as a sufficient condition for truth.[8] And since acceptability involves inductive validity, which involves right categorization, which involves entrenchment, habit must be recognized as an integral ingredient of truth. Though that may give pause, it follows as the day the night. For if we make worlds, the meaning of truth lies not in these worlds but in ourselves—or better, in our versions and what we do with them.

7. The matter is more complex than can be made clear here. Some outlines are offered in FFF, IV.

8. Pending a broadening of scope in the next paragraph, I speak here only of versions comprised of statements and only of the acceptability of what they say, without regard to other ways they symbolize or to such other considerations as relevance. Even within these limitations I am not, despite some passages in WW that suggest the contrary, proposing to *define* truth as ultimate acceptability.

So far, for simplicity, I have been speaking as if all versions consisted of statements, but actually many versions are in symbols of other kinds and in nonverbal media. Since any version may be right or wrong, though only statements are true or false, truth as rightness of what is said is a narrow species of rightness. Moreover, it is a species of but one aspect of rightness; for symbols, verbal or not, may refer not only by denotation but by exemplification or expression or by complex chains made up of homogeneous or heterogeneous referential steps, or in two or more of these ways. And a version may be right or wrong in any of these respects. A nonrepresentational painting, for instance, may exemplify certain forms and patterns, many show a way of seeing that is tested in further seeing somewhat as a proposed hypothesis is tested in further cases. The painting does not say anything, cannot be true or false, yet may be right or wrong. I cannot go into all this here, but I am convinced that philosophy must take into account all the ways and means of worldmaking.

2. ON STARMAKING

To most of what Hilary Putnam writes about *Ways of Worldmaking*,[9] I can only say "Bravo!". And while I might want to modify some passages in his paper, finding fault while saying "Bravo!" is rather awkward. More appropriate here, perhaps, is a rather general discussion of some questions commonly raised about the radical relativism with rigorous restraints and the irrealism outlined in my book.

I maintain that many world versions—some conflicting with each other, some so disparate that conflict or compatibility among them is indeterminable—are equally right. Nevertheless, right versions are different from wrong versions: relativism is restrained by considerations of rightness. Rightness, however, is neither constituted nor tested by correspondence with a world independent of all versions.

But then the objection is raised "Are the criteria of rightness

9. In "Reflections on Goodman's *Ways of Worldmaking*", *Journal of Philosophy* 76 (1979) 603–618.

themselves relative? And if so, are we not again lost in complete subjectivity?" First, note that my suggestion that permanent credibility might be taken, within certain bounds, as a sufficient condition for truth is itself credible only if credibility is no more to be equated with belief than being red is to be equated with looking red. We often believe what is not credible and disbelieve what is credible. Standards of credibility do not vary with individual opinion, over the worlds in the world of worlds sketched in *Ways of Worldmaking*. But neither are they absolute; they may vary from one world of worlds to another. Relativity goes all the way up.

"How then", comes the question, "can we ever establish anything finally and completely and for sure, even the most obvious truism and the most cherished credos?" And the answer is, of course, that we can't, and that that is no fault of mine. Neither by logic nor any other means can we prove something from nothing. We have to start with some premises and principles; and there are no absolute and incontrovertible certainties available. But that does not mean that we must start from careless guesses. We follow our confidence and convictions, which are subject to strengthening or weakening or even reversal as we strive to build right versions or worlds on the basis of these. No starting points or ending points or points along the way *are either absolute or arbitrary*. None of this is peculiar to me. But I am repeatedly forced to insist that my relativism is equidistant from intransigent absolutism and unlimited license.

Scheffler says I am ambiguous[10]—and Scheffler is an honorable man. He says I also say that worlds are other than, and answer to, right versions; and he takes the words from my own pen. And so? Do I stand guilty, then, and come before you now to bury not defend myself?

Not so. Instead, borrowing the tactics of modern diplomacy, I brazenly declare that *I am not sorry* for what I have written. Somewhat like the physicist with his field theory and his particle the-

10. In "The Wonderful Worlds of Goodman", cited in note 3 above.

ory, we can have it both ways. To say that every right version is a world and to say that every right version has a world answering to it may be equally right even if they are at odds with each other. Moreover, talk of worlds and talk of right versions are often interchangeable.

Let's begin by acknowledging that a right version and its world are different. A version saying that there is a star up there is not itself bright or far off, and the star is not made up of letters. On the other hand, saying that there is a star up there and saying that the statement "There is a star up there" is true amount, trivially, to much the same thing, even though the one seems to talk about a star and the other to talk about a statement. What is more important, we cannot find any world-feature independent of all versions. Whatever can be said truly of a world is dependent on the saying—not that whatever we say is true but that whatever we say truly (or otherwise present rightly) is nevertheless informed by and relative to the language or other symbol system we use. No firm line can be drawn between world-features that are discourse-dependent and those that are not. As I have said, "In practice, of course, we draw the line wherever we like, and change it as often as suits our purposes". If I take advantage of the privilege to speak sometimes as if there are only versions and other times as if there are worlds for all right versions, I often do it just to emphasize that point.

Scheffler also objects to the idea that we make worlds, and he is not alone in this. Much of the usual resistance can be attributed to one of two complexes. The first is the-world-is-so-wonderful-I-couldn't-do-that-well complex, otherwise known as the only-God-can-make-a-tree complex. The other is the-world-is-so-terrible-I-don't-want-to-be-blamed-for-it complex. Both rest on the fallacy that whatever we make we can make any way we like. The source of the fallacy is hard to perceive. We make chairs, computers, books, planes; and making any of these right takes skill, care, and hard work. A chair I make is likely to wobble; a book takes endless pains; I can't make a computer at all; and no one has been able to make a plane that flies far on batteries. Making right world-versions—or making worlds—is harder than making chairs or planes, and failure is common, largely because all we have available is scrap material recycled from old and stubborn worlds. Our having done no better or worse is no evidence that chairs or planes or worlds are found rather than made.

Scheffler contends that we cannot have made the stars. I ask him which features of the stars we did not make, and challenge him to state how these differ from features clearly dependent on discourse. Does he ask how we can have made anything older than we are? Plainly, by making a space and time that contains those stars. By means of science, that world (and many another) was made with great difficulty and is, like the several worlds of phenomena that also contain stars, a more or less right or real world. We can make the sun stand still, not in the manner of Joshua but in the manner of Bruno. We make a star as we make a constellation, by putting its parts together and marking off its boundaries.

In short, we do not make stars as we make bricks; not all making is a matter of molding mud. The worldmaking mainly in question here is making not with hands but with minds, or rather with languages or other symbol systems. Yet when I say that worlds are made, I mean it literally; and what I mean should be clear from what I have already said. Surely we make versions, and right versions make worlds. And however distinct worlds may be from right versions, making right versions is making worlds. This is a conspicuous case of how talk of worlds and talk of versions coalesce.

C. G. Hempel,[11] after carefully comparing my views with Otto Neurath's, urges the point that although I say that modes of organization are built into rather than found in a world, we cannot use "just any criteria we please". I agree. But his argument here is curious. He suggests an example where the measurement of the duration of an event is by the number of pulse beats of the Dalai Lama during that event. This recalls my own example of a

11. In "Comments on Goodman's *Ways of Worldmaking*", *Synthese* 45 (1980) 193–199.

frame of reference such that the motion of the earth matches the dance of Petrouchka. But whereas my example is given to stress the wide variety of conflicting right versions, his is cited against my contention that "the uniformity of nature we marvel at . . . belongs to a world of our own making"; for, Hempel says, the Dalai Lama version would not permit "the formulation of any general and reasonably simple laws of nature". Now simplicity is indeed one major criterion used in choosing among theories and thus in seeking truth; for simplification is systematization, and systematization is virtually the soul of science. But I cannot see that this in any way implies that nature apart from every version of it is simple, whatever that might mean.

Discussion of a book like *Ways of Worldmaking* often tends to focus on matters of sweeping general doctrine and venerable issues, but what I say on such matters is a by-product rather than the primary concern of the book. The main undertaking, as in *The Structure of Appearance*, is examination and comparison of the ways we make what we make—call them versions or worlds as you like—and of the criteria we use in judging what we make. Rather than argue over broad metaphysical issues, I am inclined to say "Have it your way; it matters not" (or, quoting from *Ways of Worldmaking*, "Never mind mind, essence is not essential, and matter doesn't matter"). Let's look at the ways we work, the instruments we use, and the varied and fascinating results. At the beginning of the book realism and idealism, empiricism and rationalism, and many another doctrine are dismissed in favor of what I call irrealism, which is not one more doctrine—does not say that everything or even anything is unreal—but is rather an attitude of unconcern with most issues between such doctrines. And toward the end of the book I argue that the issue between realism and idealism is undermined by the recognition that the line between convention and content is arbitrary and variable. By moving the line to one extreme or the other we get idealism or realism. I wrote:

The realist will resist the conclusion that there is no world; the idealist will resist the conclusion that all conflicting versions describe different worlds. As for me, I find these views equally delightful and equally deplorable—for, after all, the difference between them is purely conventional!

Hempel protests, asking how I can, having just rejected the distinction between content and convention, now so calmly use the term "conventional" as if it were not suspect. I do become more forgetful as time goes on, but I did not here forget from one paragraph to the next. I had hoped the reader might be stopped short by this blatant use of a term just disparaged, and be moved to ask himself how to interpret my statement. Many different interpretations of it may reflect facets of the philosophical attitude of the book. Perhaps the most straightforward way of putting it is that as the distinction between what is due to discourse and what is not flickers out, so does the significance of the issue between realism and idealism; and perhaps I should have put it that simply. But after a time, one wearies of writing flatfooted philosophy.

This brings me to one final philosophical reflection. Readers often find in my work—to their delight or disgust—many quips and cracks, puns and paradoxes, alliterations and allegories, metaphors and metonymies, synecdoches and other sins. If there are as many routes of reference as I think, perhaps some of these devices are not mere decoration or unsuccessful attempts to keep the reader awake but part and parcel of the philosophy presented and the worlds made.

While I do not know what is meant by saying that *the* world is simple or complex, I have some idea what is meant by saying that among the many worlds there are, if there are any, some are simple and some complex, some ingenuous and some ingenious, and even by saying that some are prosaic and some poetic.

3. DETERMINED MATERIALISM

The criterion of constructional definition formulated in the first chapter of *The Structure of Appearance* has gained increasing attention lately. The strong support it provides for a radical relativism has converted some former absolutists and has sent others back to rebuild their bastions.

I distinguish the general apparatus (loosely called 'logic') of a system from its special 'extralogical' terms. The general apparatus consists of basic logic together with the calculus of classes based upon membership and the calculus of individuals based upon overlapping.[12] The distinction between the general apparatus and the rest of the system is defined only by enumeration of the primitives of the general apparatus; but the principles guiding the enumeration are two. First, the general apparatus is common to all the systems under consideration; that is, each contains the basic logic and either or both of the calculi. Second, the general apparatus is schematic; something that under one system may be a part or member of another may under a different system be a whole or class containing that other. Varied embodiments leave the structure of the calculi unaltered.

Now the definitions that concerned me were all 'extralogical': introduced after the general apparatus had been fixed, and making use of at least one of the special primitives of the system. For such constructional definitions I developed a criterion in terms of extensional isomorphism, not at all meant to apply to definitions entirely in terms of the general apparatus. Thus Geoffrey Hellman's discussion of the definitions of numbers and of ordered pairs purely in terms of set theory raises no questions concerning my criterion of constructional definition and its intended application.[13]

Of course, one may seek a criterion for definitions lying entirely within the general apparatus. When Hellman comes to the definition of ordered pair, he concludes that no isomorphism criterion will work. Earlier, however, he makes a proposal for definitions of numbers that he considers "clearly within the spirit of" my criterion but that actually, I think, already forsakes isomorphism. Let me explain.

My formulation requires of the definitions of a system that there be some consistent way of replacing the ultimate factors subsumed by the extensions of the definienda so as to yield the extensions of the definientia. An ultimate factor is an individual

---

12. Obviously, other terms of these calculi may instead be taken as primitive; and the 'enumeration of primitives' mentioned in the following sentence must allow for such alternatives.

13. In "Accuracy and Actuality", *Erkenntnis* 12 (1978) 209–228.

or the null class; and replacement is consistent if the same replacement is made throughout for each such factor, different replacements for different factors, and the null class replaces itself. The set of definiens-extensions will thus reflect all such relationships as identity, nonidentity, inclusion, intersection, ordering, etc. in the set of definiendum-extensions and, since the replacements need not be ultimate factors, may introduce additional relationships.[14]

Hellman wants to relax my requirements just to the extent of allowing any replacement for the null class that does not also replace another ultimate factor. But now suppose our definienda are names of the disjoint classes A and B and of the null class C.[15] Then C is included in both A and B and no replacement for C other than C itself will preserve these inclusions. Allowing C to be replaced by something else thus sacrifices assurance of even the minimal nonsymmetric isomorphism that provides the rationale for my criterion of definition.

In his third section Hellman rather surprisingly argues that to save materialism, the criterion of definition must be strengthened rather than weakened. How can it be that a tighter, more restrictive criterion will accommodate a theory that a looser, less restrictive one will not? The basic answer, I think, is that the materialist is at heart an absolutist; he demands not merely that his own program be accepted but that alternative nonmaterialistic programs be banned. Our retreat from intensionalist and extensionalist identity criteria had the effect, indeed the purpose, of admitting for instance definitions of points in terms of lines as well as of lines in terms of points, of admitting both realistic[16] and particularistic systems, physicalistic and phenomenalistic systems, etc. But a materialism that tolerates a mentalistic alternative has lost its heart—or its spleen.

14. For example, (a,b) and (b,c) might replace f and g, introducing a new intersection.

15. Since the null class is a logical constant, this example may be oversimple, although a predicate chosen as an extralogical primitive might in fact have null extension. However, the difficulty illustrated here will also turn up in more complex cases where the null class is a member of a non-null extralogical class.

16. "Realistic" and the other terms for types of system in this sentence are used in the way defined in *SA*, IV, 4 & 5.

Under the isomorphism criterion, the set of definiens extensions must reflect and may elaborate the structure of the set of definiendum extensions but need not reflect cross-connections between definiendum and definiens extensions. For example, consider two perpendicular pairs of parallel lines, intersecting at four points. In one system, the lines are defined as pairs of collinear points; in another, the points are defined as pairs of intersecting lines. Definitions meeting the isomorphism criterion can be developed in either system for the various relations between the lines and between the points and even between the lines and the points; but the criterion is entirely noncommittal on the question whether a point 'really' is a member of a line or a line a member of a point. This obviously will not satisfy anyone who takes a firm stand on either side of that question. Likewise, neither materialists nor mentalists can abide such neutrality between their programs.

How, then, does Hellman proceed? He requires that while the structure *within* the set of definiendum extensions need only be reflected in the set of definiens extensions, certain relations between definiendum and definiens extensions must be *absolutely* preserved. In terms of our line and point example, this might mean for instance that membership of the points in the lines must be retained by the definitions as membership of the points in the lines. To say that a relation is absolutely preserved is to make a commitment: to say that the points are really members of the lines and not vice versa. Hellman does not directly require absolute preservation of the composition of the mental out of the material, but rather requires absolute preservation of some relations such as precedence between a physical and a mental event. At first sight this seems to run counter to his purpose since absolute preservation of precedence between mental and material events would seem to preclude anything like definition of either in terms of the other; but I gather that Hellman hopes that from the relations he requires to be absolutely preserved he can somehow render the mental as superfluous for materialism as lines are for the biased advocate of the point-based system of our example.

Hellman and I are in full agreement, however, that the supposed paradox or threat of 'mathematicism' or neo-Pythagorean-ism is utterly empty. The standard for judging a system—that is, what structure must be preserved, absolutely or relatively—is decided outside the system. If we decide that a system must recognize that neither do points consist of lines nor lines of points, then both of our sample systems are ruled out; and if we decide that numbers are not identical with physical objects and that a system must preserve this nonidentity, then mathematicism is ruled out. A system cannot overrule but is governed by such a decision.

The rest of Hellman's paper is concerned with seeking a possible or feasible (not obviously untenable) thesis of materialism. Although he explored adjustment of the criterion of definition to accommodate materialism, he says that materialism need not be constructional—that the slogan "no difference without a physical difference" may be taken to mean not that all differences are definable from but only that all are 'determined by' physical differences. That raises the question what constitutes 'determination': and neither Hellman, nor anyone else so far as I know, gives more than vague hints at an answer. One suspects furthermore that an interpretation general enough to license a materialistic system may also license an alternative mentalistic system. All the same, an unrepentant relativist must be impressed by how conviction here hunts for a doctrine, how the word "materialism" inspires loyalty to a thesis still wanting not only substantiation but even clear formulation.

4. WORLDS OF INDIVIDUALS

Predicates without Properties

One thread of an argument by Herbert Hochberg[17] runs somewhat as follows: that "white" applies to certain things does not make them white; rather "white" applies because they are white.

17. In "Mapping, Meaning, and Metaphysics", *Midwest Studies in Philosophy* 2 (1977) 191–211.

Plausible enough but misleading. Granted, I cannot make these objects red by calling them red—by applying the term "red" to them. But on the other hand, the English language makes them white just by applying the term "white" to them; application of the term "white" is not dictated by their somehow being antecedently white, whatever that might mean. A language that applies the term "blanc" to them makes them blanc; and a language if any that applies the term "red" to them makes them red.

Some of the trouble traces back to Alfred Tarski's unfortunate suggestion that the formula " 'Snow is white' is true if and only if snow is white" commits us to a correspondence theory of truth. Actually it leaves us free to adopt any theory (correspondence, coherence, or other) that gives " 'Snow is white' is true" and "snow is white" the same truth-value.

A second thread of Hochberg's article comes to something like this: a common predicate applies to several different things in virtue of a common property they possess. Now I doubt very much that Hochberg here intends to deny that any two or more things have some property in common; thus for him as for the nominalist there are no two or more things such that application of a common predicate is precluded. Advocates of properties usually hold that sometimes more than one property may be common to exactly the same things; but Hochberg does not seem to be urging this point either. Rather, he seems to hold that a predicate applies initially to a property as its name, and then only derivatively to the things that have that property. The nominalist cancels out the property and treats the predicate as bearing a one-many relationship directly to the several things it applies to or denotes. I cannot see that anything Hochberg says in any way discredits such a treatment or shows the need for positing properties as intervening entities.

A one-place predicate in effect sorts individuals into those it denotes and the rest. But a further question raised by Hochberg concerns many-place predicates. Surely the nominalist refuses to treat these as applying to pairs or longer sequences; for sequences, not being individuals, are for the nominalist no more admissible as denotata of predicates than are classes. The nominalist will rather construe many-place predicates as sorting and ordering individuals. While a one-place predicate classifies individuals dichotomously, a two-place predicate, for example, not only sorts out its first-place individuals and its second-place individuals, but sorts these two by two. Furthermore, if the predicate is not symmetric, so that its first-place and its second-place individuals are not all the same, it also orders some of the individuals it has thus sorted—as "above" puts *a* before *b* when "below" puts *b* before *a*.

Thus, in summary, I think that in one clear sense things are white because they are so-called, that the application of a one-place predicate to many things requires no supporting properties, and that predicates classify (and I should even say *make*) and sometimes order individuals rather than naming properties or denoting classes or sequences.

Nominalisms

In a certain village, Maria's sign reads "All clothes washed" while Anna's counters "Clothes washed in clean water". Anna always returns a wash with many articles untouched; for her spring gives clean water but not fast enough. Maria always finishes much more of a wash, but never all; for although her creek provides plenty of rather muddy water, there is always too much work to do. Whenever a traveler inquires at the inn for a laundress, he is asked whether he is a nominalist or a platonist.

Early in our association, W. V. Quine and I often discussed matters pertaining to nominalism. Nominalistic predilections had led Henry Leonard and me to develop and apply the calculus of individuals, and Quine had formulated his ontological criterion. Our common attitudes and interests soon inspired a major effort to show how nominalistic definitions could be constructed for many central concepts often cited as irredeemably platonistic.

From the beginning, our formulations of the basic principle of nominalism differed. For Quine, nominalism could countenance nothing abstract but only concrete physical objects. For me, nominalism could countenance no classes but only individuals. This difference, noted in the second paragraph of our joint paper "Steps toward a Constructive Nominalism", in no way affected our interest in or the value of the constructions undertaken in that paper.[18]

"Steps" in our view stood as something of a triumph for nominalism, since it achieved nominalistic constructions of, for instance, *proof* and *theorem*, which had always been held up as notions far beyond the nominalist's reach. But the platonist, unimpressed, simply pointed to other notions that had not yet been nominalized, and insisted on the inability of the nominalist to do everything, while the intransigent nominalist, observing that the platonist had not done and never can do everything either, went on working within his means.

Since "Steps", Quine has somewhat reluctantly adopted the platonist's luxuriant apparatus while I inch along in stubborn nominalistic austerity. Actually, the difference is not that marked; for Quine, given the chance, would gladly trade any platonistic construction for a nominalistic one, and I sometimes make use of platonistic constructions as temporary expedients awaiting eventual nominalization.

Roughly, as I have said, nominalism for Quine bars everything but physical objects, while nominalism for me bars everything but individuals; but the matter is more complex than that. A physical object is not in and by itself, apart from all systematic construction, an individual or a class or a class of classes. A football may be construed as an individual or as a class of molecules or as a class of molecule-classes of atoms, etc. Nominalism for Quine is thus better described as barring all but physical objects and *also* barring treatment of physical objects otherwise than as individuals. By now it is clear that the two restrictions are of drastically different kinds; for while the former bars entities of certain kinds, the latter rather bars certain *means of construction*. Quine's abandonment of nominalism consisted of dropping the restriction upon means of construction while retaining the restriction to physical objects.

18. *Journal of Symbolic Logic* 12 (1947) 105–122; reprinted in *PP*, pp. 173–198.

Nominalism for me admits only individuals, yet allows anything to be taken as an individual—that is, bars the composition of different entities out of the same elements. For instance, if a and b and c, whatever they may be, are taken as individuals indivisible in a given nominalistic system, then at most four other entities may be admitted under that system: those composed of a and b, of a and c, of b and c, and of a and b and c. More generally, if the number of atomic individuals in the system is n, the maximum total number of individuals in the system is $2^n - 1$. Whether the several compositions of atomic individuals are called wholes or sums or even classes does not matter, so long as no two of them contain exactly the same atoms. But once two entities made up out of the same atoms are distinguished—for example, when a and the composition of a and b are recognized as combining to make up a different entity than do b and the composition of a and b—then nominalism is violated. Platonism, using full set theory, admits a vast infinity of different entities made up out of the same atoms. Thus the restriction to individuals, even with a license to take anything as an individual, is a severe constraint.

This restriction is distinct from such other principles as finitism and particularism[19] that are perhaps no less characteristic of the nominalistic tradition. Keeping the several principles distinct matters more than deciding which deserves the name "nominalism". In my usage, the restriction to individuals is taken as the criterion of nominalism, with full recognition that nominalism seldom if ever goes by itself.

This is not the place to review the case for nominalism as set forth in "A World of Individuals",[20] but I must respond to recent questions concerning how the restrictive nominalism of that paper can be reconciled with the literal relativism of *Ways of Worldmaking*. The answer should be evident in the very formula-

19. That is, restriction to the concrete. See *SA*, pp. 104–106.
20. In *The Problem of Universals*, a symposium with Alonzo Church and I. M. Bochenski at Notre Dame University in March 1956 (Notre Dame, Ind.: University of Notre Dame Press, 1956), pp. 155–172. My paper is reprinted in *PP*, pp. 155–172.

tion of nominalism as free to take anything as an individual but not to take anything as other than an individual. My sort of relativism holds that there are many right world-versions, some of them conflicting with each other, but insists on the distinction between right and wrong versions. Nominalism, leaving choice of basis wide open, imposes a restriction on how a right version may be constructed from a basis. A right version must be well-made, and for nominalism that requires construing all entities as individuals.

Nominalism, often pronounced dead, still erupts every so often. Hartry Field in his *Science without Numbers* argues that a somewhat modified nominalism is adequate for physics.[21] David Malament, reviewing that book, comments that even if Field's constructions work for an absolutist physics, they do not work—or at least have not been shown to work—for a quantum physics.[22] Ironically, one of Quine's primary reasons for deserting nominalism seems to have been that he considers it inadequate for an absolutist physics.

21. (Princeton, N.J.: Princeton University Press, 1980).
22. *Journal of Philosophy* 79 (1982) 523–534.

III. Reference

*I*n making things we use symbols of many kinds. This chapter is concerned with symbols and their functions. "Routes of Reference" surveys briefly the ways of referring discussed in my recent books and papers. Questions on such topics as the nature of metaphor and how predicates may be split or compounded to yield predicates with different extensions are then considered. Discussion of a paper by Monroe Beardsley centers on the significance of the neglected notion of exemplificational reference. My controversial construal of depiction as a species of denotation inevitably clamors for attention. And then some fundamental questions, raised by Richard Rudner, concerning the relationship between languages and theories and concerning what is and is not involved in 'knowing a language' have to be carefully examined.

"What does a term refer to?" has a counterpart in "What is a statement about?" I examined the latter question in my paper "About" (*PP*, pp. 246–272), and some years later Joseph Ullian and I wrote a sequel, "Truth about Jones", that explores new territory: the conditions upon a statement's being true about (or false about, or speciously about) something. Beginning with some elementary observations, we soon encountered paradoxes that require intricate and complex treatment. "About Truth About", which concludes the present chapter, is an extract from that joint paper, summarizing the basic problem and a few of our simpler results.

1. ROUTES OF REFERENCE

Elementary Literal Reference

Routes of reference are quite independent of roots of reference. I am concerned here with the various relationships that may obtain between a term or other sign or symbol and what it refers to, not with how such relationships are established. And since I am thus concerned with structures rather than origins, I shall not be discussing such topics as speech-act or so-called causal theories of reference. My subject is the nature and varieties of reference, regardless of how or when or why or by whom that reference is effected.

"Reference" as I use it is a very general and primitive term, covering all sorts of symbolization, all cases of *standing for*. As a primitive relation, reference will not be defined but rather explicated by distinguishing and comparing its several forms. I use the term "denotation", somewhat more broadly than is usual, for the application of a word or picture or other label to one or many things. Denotation, itself a species of reference, has a number of subspecies differentiated in various ways. Brief descriptions of some of these subspecies follow.[1]

Verbal Denotation

This applies to those cases, such as naming, predication, description, where a word or string of words applies to one thing, event, and so on, or to each of many. "Utah" denotes a single state; "state" denotes each of fifty members of the federation; "the sun's rising" denotes each of many events; and so on. Such denotation may be more or less general, more or less vague, more or less ambiguous, and may vary with time and context. In the case of such indicator words as "here", "now", pronouns, and tensed verbs, different replicas of a term often differ in what they denote.

1. A more systematic and comprehensive treatment of all these matters is presented in Catherine Z. Elgin's *With Reference to Reference* (Indianapolis, Ind.: Hackett, 1983).

But what, if anything, does a sentence denote?[2] According to a view prevalent among logicians, a statement denotes a truth-value; that is, all true statements denote truth, and all false statements denote falsity. I dislike this on at least three scores: first, reification of truth-values (What sort of entities can truth and falsity be?); second, identification of the denotata of all true statements regardless of differences in topic (Can "Napoleon retreats" and "The sun rises" reasonably be called coextensive when "Napoleon's retreating" and "the sun's rising" denote altogether different events?); and third, lack of any provision for nondeclarative statements (What does a question or command denote?).

Perhaps the best course is to regard sentences as not strictly denoting at all. But terms or phrases or predicates often need nothing more than the addition of sentential force to become sentences; and sometimes talk of what a sentence denotes may be elliptical talk of what such a correlative expression denotes. In this elliptical sense, "The sun rises", "Does the sun rise?", "Rise, sun", and "The sun rises!" all denote the same events as "the rising sun" but are by no means coextensive with "Napoleon retreats". Nevertheless, since what predicate if any thus correlates with a given sentence may not always be evident, we must usually in careful discourse speak of what is denoted by a specific predicate rather than by a sentence.

Notation

Examples of notation are the traditional Western system for writing music and the systems devised by Rudolf von Laban and by Noa Eshkol and Abraham Wachmann for writing dance and movement in general. The difference between a verbal and a notational symbol lies not in any peculiarity of the several characters but in features of the systems in which they function. Symbols in a verbal system may be ambiguous and though syntactically distinct are not semantically distinct; that is, although verbal inscriptions and utterances classify into distinct and dis-

2. This is different from the question what a sentence is about (see *PP*, pp. 241–274) or is true about (see III,7 below).

joint characters, what one character denotes may include all or some of the things another denotes. Symbols in a notation, on the other hand, are unambiguous and both syntactically and semantically distinct.[3] A notational system must meet these requirements if it is to serve a primary function: preservation of work-identity in every chain of correct steps from score to performance and performance to score. A system violating these requirements will not guarantee that all performances in such a chain are of the same work. A notational system preserves work-identity irrespective of quality of performance.

Incidentally, a score normally lacks sentential force, serving rather as a predicate that denotes performances. But it could, indifferently, be interpreted either as a statement that certain notes and chords are related to one another in the indicated temporal order or as a command so to play or sing them.

Pictorial Denotation

This includes depiction or representation, by a drawing, painting, sculpture, photograph, film, and so on. Pictorial denotation is distinguished from notation and verbal denotation neither by the nature of the individual symbols nor, as a widely supposed, by the resemblance of the symbol to what it denotes. For resemblance is heavily dependent on custom and culture, so that whether and to what extent a symbol is 'iconic', or faithfully depicts its subject, may vary without any change in the symbol or what it denotes. A more stable and important feature of pictorial denotation is that it refers by a symbol functioning in a syntactically and semantically *dense* system—a system such that its concrete symbol-occurrences do not sort into discriminably different characters but merge into one another, and so also for what is denoted. This is not a definition of the everyday notion of pictorial representation; it does not draw quite the usual line between depiction and other varieties of denotation. It diverges, for

3. "Language" is sometimes used to cover all systems, including notations, that meet the syntactic requirements, sometimes to cover only such of these systems as are not notations. Incidentally, the standard Western system for writing music does not in all respects qualify as a notation.

example, by counting an ungraduated thermometer as depicting temperature.

Such divergence may be an acceptable price for drawing a more important and serviceable line than is drawn by ordinary usage. But the divergence can be reduced if along with density we take into account what I call *repleteness*. The symbol-system of the ungraduated thermometer then no longer qualifies as pictorial; for though dense it is of minimal repleteness in that only variations in one particular respect, height of mercury column, are significant. An undulating line charting stock market prices is likewise minimally replete and so not fully pictorial since only distance above the base, not thickness or shading, of the line matters. In contrast, when the very same line functions as a picture of mountains in a landscape, variations in many respects are significant.

Quotation

Quotation differs from other varieties of denotation in that what is quoted must be included within the quoting symbol. A quotation such as "Tom" both names and contains a particular three-letter word. The same word may be given a different name that does not contain it or may be contained in a phrase not denoting it; but in neither case is the word then quoted. Examination of how close an analogy to verbal quotation we may have in painting or music brings out plainly some fundamental differences among the three media. For painting, delicate questions arise about satisfaction of the containment but not the denotation requirement; for music, the questions are about satisfaction of the denotation rather than the containment requirement.

Thus, while description, notation, and depiction are distinguished from each other by different syntactical or semantic relationships among symbols in a system, quotation is distinguished from all of these by an additional, and nonreferential, relationship obtaining between a symbol and what it denotes.

These four familiar species of reference are not the only varieties of denotation. Some others not discussed above, such as diagraming, differ from the rest in still other ways. And all varieties of denotation together by no means exhaust elementary reference.

Exemplification

An extremely important but often overlooked form of *nondenotational* reference is exemplification: reference by a sample to a feature of the sample. A tailor's swatch, in normal use, exemplifies its color, weave, and thickness, but not its size or shape; the note a concertmaster sounds before the performance exemplifies pitch but not timbre, duration, or loudness.

Exemplification, then, far from being a variety of denotation, runs in the opposite direction, not from label to what the label applies to but from something a label applies to back to the label (or the feature associated with that label).[4] Exemplification indeed involves denotation, by inversion, yet cannot be equated with the converse of denotation; for exemplification is selective, obtaining only between the symbol and some but not others of the labels denoting it or properties possessed by it. Exemplification is not mere possession of a feature but requires also reference to that feature; such reference is what distinguishes the exemplified from the merely possessed features. Exemplification is thus a certain subrelation of the converse of denotation, distinguished through a return reference *to* denoter by denoted.

Which if any features something exemplifies often varies; ambiguity of exemplification, as of denotation, is not rare. The tailor's swatch may sometimes serve as a sample of a tailor's swatch and thus exemplify its size and shape rather than its color and texture. A stone that in a driveway refers to none of its features may in other contexts serve as a geological specimen or as an object of art, depending on which of its permanent features it exemplifies in the given context. Sometimes abstract paintings and musical works that neither represent nor express anything are extolled as "pure", as not referential at all. What matters is

---

4. In some contexts we more naturally speak of the label, in others of the feature, exemplified. The present study of routes of reference could be readily formulated in either way throughout, though as a nominalist I should want the eventual account to be free of talk of features or properties.

claimed to be the work itself, its own features, not anything beyond and referred to by it. But plainly not all the countless features of the work matter (not, for example, the painting's weighing four pounds or the symphony's being first performed during a rainstorm) but only those qualities and relationships of color or sound, those spatial and temporal patterns, and so on that the work exemplifies and thus selectively refers to, just as the swatch refers to some of its features but not others.

Elementary Nonliteral Reference

Fictive and Figurative Denotation

The varieties of reference noted above are nonfictive. But some names and descriptions and pictures—such as "Robinson Crusoe" or "winged horse" or a unicorn-picture—denote nothing although each belongs to a system along with other symbols that do denote one or many things. To hypostatize a realm of nonactual entities for these empty symbols to denote seems to me pointless and confusing. When we speak of a picture as depicting a unicorn, even though there are no unicorns to depict, what we are saying in effect is rather that the picture is a unicorn-picture; we are saying not that the picture denotes anything but rather that it is denoted by the term "unicorn-picture". And we can distinguish unicorn-pictures from centaur-pictures, as we distinguish desks from tables, with no regard to their denoting anything.

A quotation obviously cannot fail to denote; for however vacuous what is quoted may be, that must itself be contained in what quotes it. Thus "unicorn" denotes a seven-letter word even though that word denotes nothing. Although exemplification is not a denotational relation at all, we may note that a sample, like a quotation, is never empty of reference. Exemplification is never fictive—the features or labels exemplified cannot be null or vacuous—for an exemplified feature is present in, and an exemplified label denotes, at least the sample itself.

A symbol may denote metaphorically what it does not denote literally. A lake is not literally but may be metaphorically a sapphire. Literal and metaphorical denotation are alike denotation: simple application of a label to one or more things. The two are distinguished by whether the application conforms to or involves redrawing an initial classification. Metaphor arises by transferring a schema of labels for sorting a given realm to the sorting of another realm (or the same realm in a different way) under the guidance or influence or suggestion of the earlier sorting. The new sorting echoes the old and is as genuine, as 'factual', but is different.

Exemplification may be reference to what metaphorically as well as to what literally denotes, or is possessed by, a sample. And this brings us to another variety of reference: expression.

Expression

This involves exemplification of a label or feature that metaphorically rather than literally denotes or is possessed by a mark or other symbol. A symphony that expresses feelings of tragic loss does not literally have those feelings; nor are the feelings expressed those of the composer or spectator;[5] they are feelings that the work has metaphorically and refers to by exemplification. However, expression can only be placed within, not defined as, metaphorical exemplification; for a work does not express, though it may exemplify, such a metaphorical feature as having made a mint. Just as some but not all the literal properties of a painting are pictorial (involved in the functioning of the object as a painting) so some but not all the metaphorical properties are pictorial; and the work expresses such of the latter as it exemplifies.

Complex Reference[6]

So far I have been speaking in terms of simple, one-step varieties of reference, even though some of them are interrelated and dif-

5. Works of grimly depressed composers have expressed gaiety; and a work expressing bestiality may arouse disgust or horror.
6. Some of what follows is adapted from "Stories upon Stories; or, Reality in Tiers" (paper delivered at the Conference on Levels of Reality, Florence, September 1978; forthcoming in Italian in the *Proceedings* of that conference).

ferentiated in complex ways. Still to be considered are complex chains of reference made up of simple links—of one or several kinds.

Names and descriptions and depictions (that is, labels verbal and pictorial) along with what they apply to may be arrayed in a denotational hierarchy. At the bottom level are nonlabels like tables and null labels like "unicorn" that denote nothing.[7] A label like "red" or "unicorn-description" or a family portrait, denoting something at the bottom level, is at the next level up; and every label for a label is usually one level higher than the labeled label. The denotational hierarchy may be extended upward indefinitely, as by iterating quotation marks around a term or reflecting a picture in a hall of mirrors.

Denotation normally does not carry through from level to level or cut across intermediate levels: to name Piero's name is not to name Piero. But there are exceptions where a label appears at more than one level. The term "word", for instance, denotes some elements on every level, appears itself on every level but the lowest, and denotes itself as well as various names of itself. Denotational strata might thus be alternatively thought of less as levels than as layers that intersect at some places. But none of these complications or special cases need concern us much here.

Not all chains of reference run straight downward in the hierarchy. Sometimes, as we have seen, reference goes in the opposite direction: not from label to instance denoted but from instance to label or feature exemplified. I may answer your question about the color of my house by showing a sample rather than by uttering a predicate; or I may merely describe the location of the appropriate sample on a color card you have. In the latter case, the chain of reference runs down from a verbal label to an instance denoted and then up to another label (or feature) exemplified. And a picture of a bald eagle denotes a bird that may exemplify a label such as "bold and free" that in turn denotes and is exemplified by a given country. Chains of this sort, some of them longer and more complicated, are of major interest

7. The orientation here is customary but inconsequential and could be reversed or run in any direction.

when, as in these cases—unlike that of the chain from ' "Piero" '
to "Piero" to Piero—reference is transmitted from beginning to
end through the intermediate steps. The location description of
the sample refers to the color of the house via the sample; the
picture of the eagle refers to the country in question via eagles
and certain of their features. The reference by the first element to
the last in these cases is neither denotation nor exemplification
but a complex of these. Thus the eagle picture does not, in my
usage, depict the labels or properties in question although it
might be said more loosely to 'picture' them in being a picture
that, via a chain of steps, refers to them.

Referential Distance

Although a referential chain may thus wander up and down
among denotational strata, it can be treated as a linear structure
in its own right. What may for the moment be called the *referential remoteness* of an element in a chain is the number of links to
that element from the beginning of the chain. The location description of our color sample, though at the same denotational
level as the color predicate referred to, is two referential links
away from it in the given chain; and indeed, any referential chain
from an element to another at the same denotational level must
pass through at least one other denotational level. Our eagle-picture, one denotational level higher than the country referred to,
is three referential steps away from it in the given chain. The
referential remoteness of an element may vary with different
chains. But referential remoteness in a chain often—in the study
of literature, for example—has more direct interest than does
mere denotational level. What must be particularly noticed is
that an element that does not denote anything and is not even a
null label—an eagle, for example—may yet occur in a referential
chain anywhere from top to bottom.

   Although distance apart in a referential chain is one measure
of remoteness of referring element from referent, it takes no account of an important factor: the displacement that occurs in
metaphor. Whether I call a mouse a mouse or call a man a

mouse, "mouse" is just one denotational level above its referent. But the metaphorical application is against the background of the literal application and the transfer of the term to another realm: the metaphorical sorting of men under the labels "mouse", "cat", and so on reflects the literal sorting of quadrupeds under these same labels.[8] This must be taken into account by some more sensitive measure of referential remoteness. Perhaps the best course is through a correlative chain consisting entirely of links of literal reference: "mouse" denotes mice, which exemplify some such label as "timid", which also denotes and is exemplified by the man in question. Here "mouse", though only one referential step away from the mice it denotes literally, is three away from the man it denotes metaphorically. Referential remoteness is much better construed in this way.

Such correlative chains must be understood as schematic constructions, and *not by any means as providing literal translations for metaphors*. The transfer of "mouse" from mice to a man may not be via the label "timid" or any other specific predicate. Moreover, metaphorical transfer need not follow antecedently established coexemplifications of a feature or label, verbal or nonverbal; the metaphorical application itself may participate in effecting coexemplification by the mice and the man of some one or more of their common features; and just what is exemplified may be sought rather than found. Our correlative chains are merely devices for calculating referential remoteness.

We saw that metaphorical application of null labels such as "centaur" and "unicorn"—or a centaur-picture and a unicorn-picture—cannot reflect any sorting of their literal denotation, for they have none. Rather, the sorting by such null labels when they are applied metaphorically reflects the way they are themselves sorted by labels that denote and are exemplified by them. For example, "satyr" or a satyr-picture perhaps exemplifies "lasciviousness label" while "unicorn" or a unicorn-picture exemplifies "chastity label". These compound labels of labels in turn

---

8. Notice that "literal" and "verbal" are independent terms. A word is a verbal label even when used metaphorically, while even the most literal painting is nonverbal.

denote, respectively, "lascivious" and "chaste", which denote different people. The number of links in our minimal schematic correlative chain here, and thus the measure of referential remoteness of "satyr" or a satyr-picture from a man it metaphorically denotes, is three. This is the same as for the non-null label "mouse" as metaphorically denoting a man, but the pattern is different: as projected on the literal denotational hierarchy, a schematic correlative chain from "mouse" goes down to mice, up to label exemplified, and down to man denoted; the chain from "satyr" goes up to label exemplified, down to label denoted, and then down to man denoted by that label. However, minimal correlative chains are not always unique; and although there is no correlative chain from "satyr" to man that has the same pattern as the described chain from "mouse" to man, there is obviously an alternative minimal correlative chain from "mouse" to man that has the same pattern as the described correlative chain from "satyr" to man.

Allusion

The taxonomy or cartography of reference outlined here may prove helpful in the interpretation of various terms encountered in critical and other discourse. Consider two examples: "evocation" and "allusion". Evocation involves production of a feeling, memory, idea, and so on and is to that extent not a referential relation at all. But perhaps what distinguishes evocation from mere production is that the production is effected or abetted by a symbol that also refers in one way or another to what is produced. "Allusion", on the other hand, is clearly a referential term, though having different interpretations in different contexts. Sometimes it is used as a very general term virtually coextensive with "reference" itself; but such loose usage wastes a term that is better saved for some other purpose. Sometimes "allusion" is used for any reference other than simple denotation of one or more things by a given label. In other cases, it is used more narrowly for complex or indirect reference, excluding all simple, one-step reference. More narrowly still, "allusion" may be used for reference by any symbol to something at the same level in the denotational hierarchy. (Such reference will have to be complex or indirect reference via a chain passing through one or more other levels.) Or we may broaden this a little to include reference via any chain that passes more than once through any one level.

Among these alternative interpretations, we may for systematic purposes choose the one that will provide us with the most useful addition to an unambiguous vocabulary. Or we may leave "allusion" as an unsystematic term, its fickleness undisturbed, and examine on each occasion what interpretation is appropriate.

Reference and Reality

At what level, now, rides Sir Agilulf Emo Bertrandin of the Guildivern and of the Others of Corbentraz and Sura, Knight of Selimpia Citeriore and Fez?[9] The most distinctive characteristic of this hero of Italo Calvino's novel is that he does not exist; not only is he like Don Quixote a fictive character but unlike Don Quixote he does not exist according to the chronicle of his adventures. Shall we say that since he does not exist, he is on no level? Or shall we say, extending one of Calvino's jokes, that since not finding him at a level is the best evidence that he is there, he is on all levels? Let's proceed a little more slowly.

Normally the text presented would begin the referential chain; but here we find as we read that the story is supposedly written by one of the characters in it, the female knight Bradamante. So the chain in effect begins with a name of the text: the text implicitly surrounded by quotation marks. This name denotes the text itself, containing the names and descriptions of Sir Agilulf and his activities. These names and descriptions—for brevity, let "Sir Agilulf" here stand for all of them—do not denote anyone or any events literally. Yet this knight deprived of the blessings and torments of existence is, like the intrepid fighter of windmills, a vibrant symbol. That is to say, more properly, that "Sir Agilulf" and "Don Quixote" denote certain people

9. See Italo Calvino, *The Nonexistent Knight*, trans. Archibald Colquhoun (New York and London: Harcourt Brace Jovanovich, 1977).

metaphorically. Indeed, I confess that in this way I identify my-self more with these two fictive characters than with most histori-cal figures. In a correlative chain of literal reference, "Sir Agilulf" exemplifies some label of labels (say "deficient-in-humanity label") that denotes some label (say "deficient-in-humanity") that in turn denotes some human beings. "Sir Agilulf" like "Don Quixote" thus appears three links above us in a schematic correl-ative chain; but the people that "Sir Agilulf" and "Don Quixote" denote—albeit metaphorically—live on the ground with, and some of them actually *are,* you and me.

But what can flights of discourse have to do with the way any world is? Objects and events and worlds seem impervious to what we say about them and how we picture them. Am I created or destroyed or changed when someone calls me "Sir Agilulf"? Children avow a deep-seated conviction of the independence of reality from discourse when they chant "Sticks and stones will break my bones, but names will never hurt me". And the same children, some years later, will feel sure that measures of refer-ential distance from symbol to object are exclusively features of the organization of discourse, verbal or nonverbal, without effect upon reality. Are the stories upon stories we have been counting, then, merely stories, without reality?

On the contrary, I think the American system rather than the European system applies here: stories begin not one flight up but at the ground level. Any notion of a reality consisting of objects and events and kinds established independently of discourse and unaffected by how they are described or otherwise presented must give way to the recognition that these, too, are parts of the story. If we dismiss measures of referential distance as not mat-ters of fact because they are discourse dependent, we shall have trouble finding features that *are* matters of fact (see II, 1 above). Remoteness of reference is highly variable and relative; and ele-ments near each other in one chain may be far apart in another. But if these distances are nonfactual because they are thus dis-course dependent, then so also, for example, is motion. The same object may simultaneously rotate in opposite directions, dance madly, and remain at rest, depending upon the frame of refer-ence—or, better, the world-version—in question. To eliminate

67

the effects of conventions of discourse is to eliminate motion entirely—and virtually everything else. For not only the motion of objects but the objects themselves and the categories they belong to depend upon an organization effected by discourse. According to equally right accounts or depictions, a world may be made up of atoms or qualities, of ordinary objects of certain kinds or of other kinds, of riotous Soutine-like or geometric Braque-like patterns. Before me are millions of molecules or a table and chair, two successive dots flashed on a screen or one moving dot, a heterogeneous clutter of wheels and springs and screws on a watchmaker's tray or a single watch.

Yet while all features of reality are dependent upon discourse, are there perhaps some features of discourse that are independent of reality—the differences, for example, between the ways two discourses may say exactly the same thing? The old and ugly notion of synonymy rattles a warning here: Can there ever be two different discourses that say exactly the same thing in different ways, or does every difference between discourses make a difference in what is said? Luckily, we can pass over that general question here. We are concerned only with the specific question whether organization into referential chains and levels is purely conventional, independent of everything beyond discourse. And the plain answer is that such organization of discourse participates notably in the organization of a reality. A label in any non-null application, literal or metaphorical, marks off entities of a certain kind; and even where the denotation is null, the label marks off labels of a certain kind that apply to that label. Just such marking off or selection of entities and relevant kinds *makes them such* as distinguished from the results of alternative organizations. Longer referential chains effect more complex organization. Metaphorical application of "rhinoceros" to certain people picks out a significant relevant kind that cuts across familiar literal classifications. And a correlative chain of literal links here relates the new sorting of people to an old sorting of quadrupeds via labels or features that are coexemplified by, or at least have as common instances, both literal and metaphorical rhinoceroses. In the denotational hierarchy and in chains of reference lie parts of the structures of any worlds we have.

None of this, of course, identifies symbols in general with their referents. A baseball but not a "baseball" can be knocked for a home run; and indeed, a link in a referential chain normally joins two different elements. But every reality is nevertheless dependent on right discourse; and every right discourse is dependent on a reality that is dependent on discourse.

Sir Agilulf serves also as a trenchant metaphor for the so-called real world. As he cannot be separated from armor, a world cannot be separated from versions. The armor may be changed, a new version may replace an old; but as we cannot find Sir Agilulf apart from all armor, we cannot find a world apart from all versions. The metaphor can be carried further. When Sir Agilulf dies, his armor is a heap on the ground. A version may collapse, too: encounter difficulties it cannot overcome, and stop working.

My multimedia *Hockey Seen: A Nightmare in Three Periods and Sudden Death*[10] provides some nonverbal illustrations of kinds of reference described above. The second period is a fast, high-energy movement based on the swift actions and conflicts of the game. The referee's struggle to keep things under control is a major theme in this period. He starts and stops the play, separates fighting players, banishes some to the penalty box, and signals to players and watchers the infractions committed and the consequent penalties. At one point he performs a solo dance based on these signals.

In terms of the types of reference distinguished above, this period denotes—depicts, represents—incidents in a hockey game; not incidents in any particular game, but incidents common to hockey games. Representation, contrary to a prevalent opinion, may be either particular, as in a portrait, or general, as in the eagle-picture in a dictionary.

The work as a whole, however, depicts neither any particular hockey game nor hockey games in general but is rather, like a

---

10. First performed in 1972 and 1973 in Cambridge, Mass., and most recently, in August 1980 in Knokke, Belgium, sponsored by the Belgian Radio-Television system in conjunction with the Ghent University conference *Art in Culture.* Drawings by Katharine Sturgis; author and producer, Nelson Goodman; choreographer, Martha Gray; composer, John C. Adams.

centaur-picture, a fictive representation. We often say that such a representation depicts a game or an animal that never did and never will exist. Less inconsistently, we may say that the picture or the dance does not represent or denote at all but is *denoted* by such a predicate as "centaur-picture" or "hockey-representation".

Of greater import, the work *exemplifies*, as does a purely abstract dance, certain movements and patterns of movement, changes of pace and direction, configurations and rhythms. Many of these are derived from both the action of hockey and the vocabulary of dance, but the reference by the work to such properties is a matter of exemplification not representation.

Moreover, the second period *expresses* various aspects of competition, conflict, violence, frustration, and the struggle between aggression and authority. These properties are not literally exemplified: no fights, no defeat or victory, no punishment, no (intended) violence or injury occur on the stage. These are properties possessed metaphorically, and referred to, by the work, and thus expressed by it. The slow-motion third period, with all the players wearing goal-tender's masks, expresses taut and long-drawn defensive tensions and perhaps an effort, by means of fearsome visages, to fend off an unknown fate.

The three elementary species of reference—denotation, exemplification, and expression—often interact. The representation of hockey affects the way the action is organized in our perception, and this influences the features that the work comes to exemplify and express. Much the same action, divorced from the reference to hockey, might be seen as exemplifying and expressing quite other properties. Furthermore, reference is often through chains such that each link is reference of one or another of the three elementary types. For example, the work represents hockey, which in itself exemplifies ferocity of competition. Thus the representation of hockey refers, via hockey, to such ferocity. This indirect reference is not itself denotation or exemplification or expression but a complex of the first two and is altogether different from the direct expression of the same ferocity—an expression that may be missing from an ineffectual work or a list-less performance.

I hope these examples will suggest how the comparative study of routes of reference enables us to understand better not only our critical and theoretical discourse but also how, by means of many symbol systems and functions, we create and comprehend the worlds we live in.

2. METAPHOR AS MOONLIGHTING

Recently in a number of symposia we have evidence of a growing sense that metaphor is both important and odd—its importance odd and its oddity important—and that its place in a general theory of language and knowledge needs study.

Metaphorical use of language differs in significant ways from literal use but is no less comprehensible, no more recondite, no less practical, and no more independent of truth and falsity than is literal use. Far from being a mere matter of ornament, it participates fully in the progress of knowledge: in replacing some stale 'natural' kinds with novel and illuminating categories, in contriving facts, in revising theory, and in bringing us new worlds. The oddity is that metaphorical truth is compatible with literal falsity;[11] a sentence false when taken literally may be true when taken metaphorically, as in the case of "The joint is jumping" or "The lake is a sapphire."

The oddity vanishes upon recognition that a metaphorical application of a term is normally quite different from the literal application. Applied literally, the noun "sapphire" sorts out various things including a certain gem but no lake; applied

11. "Metaphorical truth" does not mean that the truth of the sentence is metaphorical but that the sentence taken metaphorically is true. The same sort of ellipsis is to be understood in many like locutions. In what follows I have usually avoided the confusing word "meaning"; and for readers not familiar with philosophical terminology, I have ordinarily written "application" rather than "extension" for the collection of things denoted by a word or other label. I have also often kept clear of an ambiguity of "use" by writing either "application" or "function" as the case may be.

metaphorically (in the way here in question) it sorts out various things including a certain lake but no gem. "The lake is a sapphire" is thus literally false but metaphorically true, while "Muddy Pond is a sapphire" is both literally and metaphorically false. Metaphorical truth and falsity are as distinct from—and as opposite to—each other as are literal truth and falsity. And "The lake is a sapphire" is metaphorically true if and only if "The lake is metaphorically a sapphire" is literally true.

Obviously, metaphor and ambiguity are closely akin in that ambiguous terms likewise have two or more different applications. But metaphor differs from ambiguity in that a literal application precedes and influences a correlative metaphorical application. Words often have many different metaphorical as well as many different literal applications. In an ironic metaphorical use, "Muddy Pond is a sapphire" is true, while "The lake is a sapphire" is false. The two metaphorical applications here derive in different ways from the literal application of "sapphire" to gems.

Donald Davidson disputes this straightforward account, denying that a term may have a metaphorical application different from its literal one, and scorning the notions of metaphorical truth and falsity.[12] A sentence is true or false, he maintains, only as taken literally; to take a literally false sentence metaphorically is not to take it as saying something else that may be true, but merely to bring out certain suggestions of that false sentence, to invite comparisons or evoke thoughts or feelings. What can be said for this position?

The acknowledged difficulty and even impossibility of finding a literal paraphrase for most metaphors is offered by Davidson as evidence that there is nothing to be paraphrased—that a sentence says nothing metaphorically that it does not say literally, but rather functions differently, inviting comparisons and stimulating thought. But paraphrase of many literal sentences also is exceedingly difficult, and we may seriously question whether any sentence can be translated exactly into other words in the same or any other language. Let's agree, though, that literal

12. In "What Metaphors Mean", *Critical Inquiry* 5 (1978) 31–47.

paraphrase of metaphor is on the whole especially hard. That is easily understood since the metaphorical application of terms has the effect, and usually the purpose, of drawing significant boundaries that cut across ruts worn by habit, of picking out new relevant kinds for which we have no simple and familiar literal descriptions. We must note in passing, though, that the metaphorical application may nevertheless be quite clear. For just as inability to define "desk" is compatible with knowing which articles are desks, so inability to paraphrase a metaphorical term is compatible with knowing what it applies to. And whether a man is metaphorically a Don Quixote or a Don Juan is perhaps even easier to decide than whether he is literally a schizoid or a paranoiac.

In a second argument, Davidson considers the example of a term, "burned up", that after being used metaphorically loses its metaphorical force through overuse. His argument runs somewhat as follows: "burned up" does not change its application when it ceases to be metaphorical; what is lost is the way it functions in inviting comparisons between angry people and things consumed by flame; and this shows that metaphor is a matter of function rather than of application. Now I agree that when a metaphor wilts, it no longer instigates such comparison—comparison, I would say, between two different applications of the term. But Davidson's argument seems at odds with his thesis that the metaphorical and literal applications of a term cannot be different. For if when "burned up" becomes a literal term for angry people, it has the same application as when metaphorical, then its metaphorical application must have been different from its other (original) literal application to things consumed by flame. When "burned up" retires as a metaphor, it becomes ambiguous; one literal application no longer suggests or is influenced by the other, but neither one is newly established.

Incidentally, if "burned up" retains its metaphorical application when its metaphorical force vanishes and is, as Davidson claims, in that application coextensive with "angry", we may well ask: Why, then, is there any difficulty about paraphrasing "burned up" when metaphorical by "angry"? I think that "burned up" was an effective metaphor in being not quite coextensive with "angry"; that, for example, "burned up" and "came to a boil" did not apply metaphorically in exactly the same cases; and that for a while after the metaphor fades, the second literal application of "burned up" still departs somewhat from that of "angry". Of course, as with words in general, such differences tend to rub off with frequent careless use.

Davidson, in a further argument, cites T. S. Eliot's "The Hippopotamus" to show that a nonmetaphorical text can invite comparison as pointedly as does a metaphor. That seems obvious enough also from simpler examples. The nonmetaphorical sentences "Compare the True Church with the hippopotamus" and "The True Church has important features in common with the hippopotamus" are quite as explicit invitations as the metaphorical "The True Church is a hippopotamus"; and in general, metaphorical and nonmetaphorical sentences alike can be put to such uses as inviting, warning, shocking, enticing, misleading, inquiring, informing, and persuading. Plainly, then, no such function is peculiar to metaphor, and metaphor cannot be defined in terms of the performance of, or the capacity to perform, any such function. Davidson's argument here seems a conclusive refutation of his own thesis.

Metaphor in my view involves withdrawing a term or rather a schema of terms from an initial literal application and applying it in a new way to effect a new sorting either of the same or of a different realm. Davidson's denial that the metaphorical and literal applications of a term can be distinct and that a statement false when taken literally may be true when taken metaphorically seems to me to constitute a fundamental confusion about metaphor.

As Ted Cohen has often stressed,[13] and as I illustrated in *Languages of Art*[14] by the case of a picture that is both metaphorically and literally blue, a metaphorical truth is not always a literal

13. For example, "Notes on Metaphor", *Journal of Aesthetics and Art Criticism* 34 (1976) 358–359.

14. Page 83. However, in some other passages in that book, I have not taken this sufficiently into account. For further interesting discussion of this and related matters, see Israel Scheffler's *Beyond the Letter* (London: Routledge & Kegan Paul, 1979).

falsehood. Wherein then, Cohen asks in effect, lies the metaphorical character of the literally true "No man is an island"? Quite clearly, the metaphorical reading is different from the literal one: in the metaphorical reading, a schema of terms that taken literally sort geographical units is applied to sorting organisms, with the result that no men fall under "island". "No man is an island" is metaphorical insofar as it implicitly continues "rather, every man is part of a mainland". Likewise "No lake is a ruby" is as metaphorical as "That lake is a sapphire"; for in both cases a schema of terms for sorting jewels is being applied to bodies of water.

Furthermore, as shown by our doubly blue picture, a literal extension of a term and a correlative metaphorical extension need not be altogether separate; they may, though different, have items in common. Although "blue" applies both literally and metaphorically to the picture in question, many other things that are either literally or metaphorically blue in this way are not both.

But what if all and only things literally blue were also metaphorically blue? Still the distinction between literal and metaphorical use, in the face of extensional equivalence, will not require resort to nonextensional "meanings" or "senses". Difference in meaning between two extensionally equivalent terms amounts to difference between their secondary extensions—that is, the extensions of parallel compounds of those terms. For example, although all and only unicorns are centaurs, not all and only (or indeed many) unicorn-pictures are centaur-pictures; and although all and only featherless bipeds are laughing animals, not all and only featherless-biped descriptions are laughing-animal descriptions. Likewise, when a literal and a correlative metaphorical use coincide extensionally, the significant difference is between secondary extensions: the literally-blue descriptions (descriptions as literally blue) are not all and only the metaphorically-blue descriptions (descriptions as metaphorically blue).[15]

15. On the notion of secondary extensions and parallel compounds, see my "On Likeness of Meaning" and "Some Differences about Meaning" in PP, pp. 221–238; see also pp. 204–206. As Israel Scheffler has pointed out to me, I

Ordinarily, I have said, a term effects a literal sorting that upon metaphorical transfer is reflected in a new sorting. But where a term with a null literal extension—a term such as "unicorn" that does not apply literally to anything—is applied metaphorically, the new sorting cannot thus reflect any literal sorting by that term. Here again, secondary extensions are involved. The metaphorical sorting reflects, rather, the literal sorting of descriptions that is effected by such a compound of the term as "literally-unicorn description (or picture)".

A different and curious case is cited above (III,1) where I suggested that Italo Calvino's Sir Agilulf is, among other things, a metaphor for 'the real world': just as the mythical knight existed only in and as some sort of armor, the chimerical one-real-world exists only in various versions. But how can a literally null term have a different, metaphorical application that is also null, since there is at most one null extension? The answer is that there are many null labels—that is, labels with null extension—and that the compound term "Sir Agilulf description", taken literally, sorts out certain from other null labels. This sorting is reflected in the sorting of one-real-world descriptions from other null labels when we take "Sir Agilulf" to be a metaphor for the non-existent one-real-world.

Such special cases, though, must not leave the impression that metaphor is a mere literary luxury, a rare or esoteric or purely decorative device. By so putting old words to new work, we save enormously on vocabulary and take advantage of established habits in the process of transcending them. Metaphor permeates nearly all discourse; thoroughly literal paragraphs without fresh or frozen metaphors are hard to find in even the least literary texts. In terms of multiple application of words—and other symbols—and of schemata consisting of them, we can understand

---

assume here that the modifiers "literally" and "metaphorically" are incorporated in the original terms; otherwise, an intermediate step is needed. Incidentally, were "literally blue" and "metaphorically blue" coextensive, there might also be this further difference: that the sorting of pictures by feeling under color terms might still differ from the literal sorting under these terms in what falls under some term other than "blue".

how various figures of speech are related to each other and to literal discourse, and also how metaphor constitutes so economical, practical, and creative a way of using symbols.

In metaphor, symbols moonlight.

3. SPLITS AND COMPOUNDS

Rolf Eberle makes a sound effort to develop and extend the line of thought in my papers on meaning. Some of the points he raises have been, at least in part, anticipated in a paper by Richard Wollheim[16] and in my reply to that paper (IV, 8 below).

In "On Likeness of Meaning" and "Some Differences about Meaning" (*PP*, pp. 221–238), as well as in *Languages of Art,* I called such predicates as "picture of Pegasus" (or "Pegasus-picture") and "Pegasus-description" *unbreakable.* Wollheim rightly objected, and I responded that the more appropriate term is *one-place.* I insist only that such predicates cannot be treated as two-place, with the names occupying quantifiable places so that we can infer that there is such a thing as Pegasus or Pickwick. But the one-place predicates may nevertheless, without harm and to some purpose, be split. "Picture of Pegasus" may be split into "picture" (applying to all pictures) and "of Pegasus"(applying to pictures and descriptions of Pegasus). "Picture of Pegasus" has as its extension the intersection of the extensions of the two predicates it has been split into; and from

> k is a picture of Pegasus

we can infer both

> k is a picture

and

> k is of Pegasus.

So much was already covered in the exchange with Wollheim. Since then, as the result partly of correspondence with Michael

---

16. Rolf A. Eberle, "Goodman on Likeness and Differences of Meaning", *Erkenntnis* 12 (1978) 3–16; Wollheim, "Nelson Goodman's Languages of Art", *Journal of Philosophy* 67 (1970) 531–539.

Root[17] and partly of consideration of the Eberle paper, I have been reminded that one-place predicates of the kind in question can be split in more than one way. From "picture of Pegasus" or "picture of a unicorn" we may rather split off "picture of (a)" (applying to all representational pictures). This is a splitting *off* rather than a splitting into, since the remainder—"Pegasus" or "centaur"—does not stand as a separate predicate applying to anything but rather as a dependent modifier restricting the split-off predicate so that the whole applies only to Pegasus-pictures or centaur-pictures.

Alternatively, we may even split off two one-place predicates from the whole: "picture" and "of (a)". Now "of a", applying here to all descriptions and representational pictures coincides, I take it, with Eberle's "representative". In this splitting off, the remainder again serves as a dependent modifier. Accordingly, and in keeping with what Eberle says, the extensional relationships involved may be diagramed as in Figure 3.

Different splittings serve different purposes; no one of them is exclusively correct or preferred. Root pointed out to me that the splitting into "picture" and "of Pegasus" does not disclose, as is required for the analysis of likeness of meaning in my paper, that "picture of Pegasus" is a compound of "Pegasus". For that, the appropriate alternative splitting is into "picture of" and the dependent modifier "Pegasus".

This answers persistent complaints that treating predicates of the kind in question as one-place deprives us of legitimate inferences and burdens us with countless unrelated predicates; for recognizing that these one-place predicates are nevertheless divisible as illustrated enables us to take account of relationships between "unicorn-picture" and "centaur-picture" and of these to "picture" and to "of a". And in reply to the protest made long ago by Alonzo Church and pressed often since by others, lion-huntings and tiger-huntings, even in Antarctica, make up different kinds of subclasses of huntings—subclasses marked off by using "lion" and "tiger" as modifiers restricting "hunting".

17. Correspondence of October 1976, referred to with his permission.

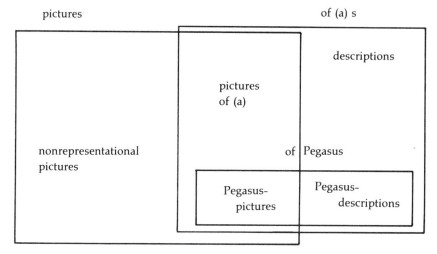

Figure 3.

Earlier I was inclined to admit among the compounds of a term every word or phrase that incorporated it (so that "battle", say, would count as a compound of "bat") since this seems harmless. But plainly the only compounds relevant to meaning are such that the term compounded (say, "unicorn") serves as modifier of the compounding addition (say, "picture of a"). These obviously differ significantly from such cases as addition of the prefix "deter" to "gent" or "mine"; for "detergent" and "determine" hardly pick out subclasses of things that deter.

All this, I think, is quite compatible with Eberle's ideas, and with the interesting analysis he develops in terms of quasi-meanings. He is of course correct in reminding us that a description of a description of k is not a description of k, and I have pointed out elsewhere (WW, III, 2) that even a picture of a picture of k is not always a picture of k. Under "secondary extension" I have usually lumped all nonprimary extensions, but these may be sorted into (properly) secondary, tertiary, and so on extensions. However, with only properly secondary extensions and even with only descriptions, the result that no two terms have the same meaning was forthcoming. That, though, was neither an objective of my papers nor a result that may not be modified by imposing some more or less reasonable restriction, such as to ways of compounding that do not give different secondary extensions for every two terms (*PP*, p. 238).

4. REFERENCE IN ART

Monroe Beardsley presents a compendium of comment ranging from considered formulations of prevalent criticisms to some acute new questions.[18] He is quite correct in urging that the relation between a picture and what it represents differs in important respects from the relation between a term or description and what it applies to or describes, notably in that words may combine with other words to make statements while pictures do not so combine either with other pictures or with words. Thus a term *T* applies to *a* if and only if *"Ta"* is true, while we have no analogue in the case of a picture. But that difference does not seem to me to obscure the common function of description and depiction as denotation in different kinds of symbol systems. To take denotation as dependent upon and arising from declaration is entirely gratuitous. Much as "bright star", quite apart from its incorporation in statements, applies to certain objects—and "Babe Ruth hitting a homer" applies to certain events, and "Churchill" to a certain person—pictures of stars or of Babe Ruth hitting a home or of Churchill apply to these objects or events or that person. A picture of pears no less than the word "pears" applies to what is in or is to be put in the jar. Again, a musical score, as I see it, applies to performances in much the same way and is equally indifferent as between statement and command (*LA*, pp. 153, 199-200). This common relationship of applying to or standing for, I call *denotation*—not to preclude but rather to introduce examination of various types of denotation in different symbol systems and also the relationships between denotation and other types of reference.

To Beardsley's proposal to distinguish depiction—or what we usually consider to be 'naturalistic' or 'realistic' representation—in terms of resemblance between picture and pictured, I have lit-

18. In *"Languages of Art and Art Criticism"*, *Erkenntnis* 12 (1978) 95-118.

tle objection so long as we bear in mind that resemblance is a variable and relative matter that as much follows as guides customs of representation.

On the other hand, I disagree entirely with Beardsley's contention that pictures cannot refer generally. The eagle-picture in the dictionary is of no particular eagle or of eagles of a given species but of eagles in general. In Figure 4 we have two pictures, one a dog-picture, the other a cat-picture. Neither represents any particular animal nor any particular species of dog or of cat.

Beardsley's insistence that:

The smew picture that accompanies the definition of "smew" in my dictionary cannot denote smews in general, for it depicts a smew with seven slanting black stripes on its right side, and if there are smews with fewer or more, it is not true of (applicable to) them.

would seem to suggest that every zebra-picture is a picture of a particular zebra with a specific number (say 35½?) stripes; and I doubt that under the implied requirement any picture made of my Dalmatian—even a photograph—had the right number of spots to count as a picture of him. Beardsley's sentence:

Of course, it might be made, or understood, to refer to all smews by arbitrary convention; but if it is a character in a symbol system whose semantic rules determine its reference, then if it denotes at all, we must read it as denoting seven-striped smews.

suggests a puzzling distinction between arbitrary conventions and semantic rules. Nor can I discern the grounds for or the import of his statement that the smew picture must refer indefinitely to 'a smew' rather than generally to smews.

Beardsley is much interested in exemplification. He is fascinated by and suspicious of it; and his attitude seems to alternate between affection and aversion. His comments on it range, in my opinion, from quite right to quite wrong.

First, he is quite right in calling me to account for misapplying the term "exemplification" in certain cases that amount only to instantiation. To say that a picture is of a certain kind—say a Churchill-picture or a centaur-picture—is not to say that the picture exemplifies but only that it instantiates a label for, or possesses the property of being such a picture. Exemplification, as I have emphasized, coincides not with the converse of denotation but with a proper subclass of that converse: the subclass consisting of those cases where what is denoted or possesses refers back as a sample, to what denotes or is possessed. But my admission of error in using the term "exemplification" in one passage ·carries with it no retraction or modification of theory; and, indeed, Beardsley's noticing my mistake shows that he understands exemplification better than he realizes.

I cannot at all go along with Beardsley's frequent feeling that the whole idea of exemplification might be dropped without loss—that mere possession may be all that matters. Let me argue my point here by working backward. Beardsley will surely grant that a work does not express all the properties it possesses; and on the whole he seems not to object to my theory of expression or offer any alternative. He seems to agree that what is expressed is metaphorically possessed; and, rather obviously, to express is to refer in some way to what is expressed. Thus Beardsley's objection cannot be that the idea of reference by a work to some of its properties is itself untenable, but rather that the distinction between the literal properties that are exemplified and those that are merely possessed is unclear or irrelevant for works of art.

He stresses, for instance, the fact that "exemplify", unlike "express", is not a normal part of the critic's vocabulary. Granted. "Exemplify" belongs, rather, to a theoretic vocabulary that may be used in describing and analyzing the critic's practice. Whether or not the critic uses the terms "denotes", "depicts", "exemplifies", "expresses", etc., he concentrates on what a work symbolizes or refers to in one or more of these ways. And a critic who focuses on properties that are possessed but not exemplified is as far afield as a tailor who discusses materials in terms of the size, shape, absolute weight, etc. of his swatches. The tailor or the critic may call attention to some properties that are merely possessed—the inconvenient smallness of a swatch, or the artist's depression at the time of production[19]—as an aid to the understanding of how the swatch is serving as a sample, or the painting functioning as a work of art, rather than as just a piece of colored cloth.

Beardsley protests that while the distinction between the properties a swatch is and is not a sample of is clearly established by long practice, the distinction between what a work does and does not exemplify is not nearly so well established or easy to discern. Discovery of what a poem or painting exemplifies may often, though not always, take time, training, and even talent; but that only shows that works of art usually exemplify more subtly than do tailor's swatches. When determination of what a given term denotes or a given picture depicts or a given face expresses gives us trouble, we do not at once conclude that the symbol in question fails to denote or depict or express, much less that the whole idea of denotation or depiction or expression is empty.

In passing, Beardsley argues further that in the case of a work of art there is nothing comparable to the bolt of cloth that a swatch is snipped from. But that is beside the point. Samples, even in the clearest and most commonplace contexts, are not necessarily bits of a batch. The chip on a paint manufacturer's color card is a sample of the color in question, if it matches nearly enough, even if produced by printer's inks. The birthday cake in the baker's window is a sample of certain of its properties whether or not any other such cakes are ever ordered or baked.

Beardsley quite justly complains, however, that I have sometimes mistakenly associated exemplification with emphasis. Works of art, like tailor's swatches, may indeed exemplify some

19. The work obviously does not possess the artist's mood, but does possess the property of having been produced by the artist when depressed.

of their least and not some of their most conspicuous properties. Swatches cut doughnut-shaped would powerfully attract attention to their shape without exemplifying it, while they might exemplify properties of luster, resilience, etc. discernible only through intensive examination. Likewise, a quartet that is notably loud or fast or slow may exemplify none of these properties but instead some intricate rhythmic or melodic pattern; and a painting that is obtrusively huge is less likely to exemplify that property than, say, certain color relationships in bands of different widths. Any prominence an exemplified property has may arise from rather than give rise to exemplification.

Beardsley apparently finds exemplification the most unsettling matter in what he calls an unsettling book, and he is persistently seeking further clarification. If he is asking for general instructions how to determine what a work exemplifies, I shall defer my reply until he gives general instructions for determining what a work describes or represents. If he is objecting that while he can at least readily tell in particular cases what a text describes or a painting depicts or a quartet expresses he cannot tell what any of them exemplifies, perhaps he is letting the terminology get in his way. Surely he does not suppose that critical comment consists of random listing of properties a work possesses, or that understanding a work amounts to noting such properties indiscriminately. A vital part of aesthetic understanding, especially but not exclusively in the case of abstract works, is determining which among its properties the work not only possesses but also *conveys*. The significant properties of a work, we might say, are those it signifies. This must be taken fully into account in one way or another, and my way is in terms of exemplification. Beardsley offers no alternative.

In contending that aesthetic experience is cognitive, I am emphatically not identifying it with the conceptual, the discursive, the linguistic. Under "cognitive" I include all aspects of knowing and understanding, from perceptual discrimination through pattern recognition and emotive insight to logical inference. Beardsley's grasp of this point is rather wavering. He seems to forget it entirely when he writes "some critics have asked of Dubuffet that he 'reflect the most ominous aspects of our time', others have praised his art for being 'compassionate and gentle', with no suggestion of cognitive claims." Discerning that a work is compassionate and gentle is for me as much a cognitive matter as is perceiving it to reflect aspects of our time. Again, Beardsley balks at my saying that a late Rembrandt self-portrait can make manifest fresh and significant relationships. But Beardsley knows as well as I that after a couple of hours at an exhibition we often step out into a visual world quite different from the one we left. We see what we did not see before, and see in a new way. We have *learned.*

Cognition of any kind involves discovery; and the weight I give to this aspect of aesthetic experience seems to Beardsley incompatible with the classic aesthetic virtues of unity, balance, and vitality. I cannot see why. What counts is how these qualities are realized. Achieved by trivial or humdrum means, they are of little aesthetic interest. Achieved in subtle or novel ways or against odds, they may contribute to aesthetic excellence; but then invention, discovery, cognition, is involved. And incidentally I am not sure, especially in view of the recent history of art, that disunity, imbalance, and morbidity may not claim some aesthetic value.

Although these notes do not cover all that Beardsley has written, I hope they may help resettle the dean of American aesthetics.

In the development of my theory of symbols, notation occupies a prominent place, and in music we find the most familiar examples of notation in the arts. As a result, much of what I say about music happens to be about notation, and this may easily create a false impression. Jens Kulenkampff does well to point out that in my view notation is not music, a musical score is not a musical work, and the major aesthetic characteristics of music are not to be understood in terms of the characteristics of notational sumbols. The musical work consists of performances, and these usually function in art and in worldmaking quite differently from a score.

Kulenkampff[20] quotes and discusses a paragraph in *Languages of Art* where I say that a performance of a musical work under standard notation, if denotative at all, is descriptive rather than representational because it is in a syntactically differentiated system. As a result of conversations with Vernon Howard and further thought, I see that this needs some modification. Considered solely with respect to properties prescribed in the score— the properties that are common to all (correct) performances of the work—a performance does belong to a syntactically and semantically articulate system wherein certain sounds or ranges of sound are uniquely correlated with the characters in the score. But while compliance with a score identifies a performance as of a given work, a performance ordinarily functions within the full spectra of sound; that is, within a dense system such that every difference in sound—whether between correct performances or between correct and incorrect performances— makes a difference. If a performance functioning in this way denotes, it is thus representational rather than descriptive. Of course it often also or instead exemplifies or expresses in other systems.

Kulenkampff is also concerned to bring out the way music participates in worldmaking. How representational painting makes worlds is strikingly clear to anyone who has stepped into a new world after seeing an exhibition of works that work. Abstract paintings, by exemplification and expression, recombine and reweight properties and can make everything we see "square off into geometric patches or swirl in circles or weave into textural arabesques" (*WW*, p. 105). Nondenotational music operates in similar fashion with auditory properties, but not with auditory properties exclusively; for what we hear may exemplify properties of what we see. An auditory and a visual event may both literally exemplify a pattern of highly contrasting multiple elements, or metaphorically exemplify conflict; and a "poem, a painting, and a piano sonata may literally and metaphorically exemplify some of the same features" (*WW*, p. 106).

20. Jens Kulenkampff, "Music Considered as a Way of Worldmaking", *Journal of Aesthetics and Art Criticism* 39 (1981) 254–258.

5. DEPICTION AS DENOTATION

In a searching and original paper, Jenefer Robinson examines the relation between representation and reference.[21] Such lucid writing often casts a perhaps unintentionally harsh light on some of the views it discusses. The miscalled 'causal' (better, 'historical') theory of reference seems to wilt to the unexceptionable and unexceptional doctrine that a term denotes what it does because it is so used. And if Frege's seemingly contrasting view is that a term denotes what it does because of its sense, we want to ask why it has the sense it has—other than through being so used. But these remarks are mine, not Robinson's, and are admittedly prejudiced and uninformed on the theories of meaning in question.

I am impressed by her questions concerning how Frege's theory can deal with metaphor, and Saul Kripke's with fictive representation; and I have no idea how proponents of these theories might answer. Her detailed discussion of the virtues and defects of the two theories of meaning as ways of accounting for representation, fictive representation, and representation-as I find illuminating and generally convincing.

Her statement, "For a picture to represent the queen there must be a mapping from its pictorial properties to the represented properties of the queen", is, indeed, rather unguarded; for unless we put some restraints on the kind of mapping or the system in question, there will be some mapping from the same picture to any other subject as well. Later, however, she does stress dependence on context. We must not forget that only relative to a given system does the picture represent the queen; and to say without qualification that the picture represents the queen is tacitly to say that it represents the queen relative to the system in question in the given context.

Robinson's comments concerning the treatment of representation in *Languages of Art* are brief and rather indirect. Near the beginning of her paper she writes that for present purposes

21. "Two Theories of Representation", *Erkenntnis* 12 (1978) 37–53.

she is going to accept my statement that a picture that represents an object must refer to it. At the end, she suspects that representation and representation-as cannot be entirely explained as species of reference. I can see why. Literal representation of an actual subject can, I think, be explained as denotation—under a slightly broadened interpretation of "denotation"—by a picture functioning in a symbol system of a certain kind. On the other hand, representation-as and fictive representation are matters not of what a picture denotes but of what labels of certain sort denote the picture; the difference from ordinary representation is in direction rather than kind of reference. Representation, representation-as, and fictive representation can all be explained *in terms of,* rather than *as,* species of reference.

Søren Kjørup writes that he has no quarrel with my theory of representation but wants to "expand and reformulate it".[22] His effort seems to me more a matter of supplementation; and since I am often accused of overlooking the fact that only as the result of a user's acts and intentions does a symbol refer at all and refer to what it refers to, I should say once more that my apparent neglect is itself intentional. Of course a mark or a painting becomes a symbol, as a piece of wood becomes a railroad tie, through actual or intended use, whether by people, other animals, or machines;[23] but the characteristics and functions of symbols as of railroad ties can be studied quite apart from the acts or beliefs or motives of any agent that may have brought about the—referential or mechanical—relationships involved. In my approach to a theory of symbols I have examined types of referential functions and systems, willingly leaving to others questions about who perpetrated the systems and why. The radical version of speech-act theory that Kjørup sets forth when he writes: "To refer is to perform an act of a very special kind—and acts can only be performed by conscious human beings" seems to me

22. In "Pictorial Speech Acts", same, pp. 55–71.
23. To grant that a word's reference may depend on its use does not of itself require that that use be by humans or that the use be intended rather than accidental.

quite wrong. The bullet as well as the gunman kills; the shell on the beach, and not anyone at all, cuts my foot; and I need not ask who bounced the ball, or whether it just rolled off the shelf, to know the way the ball bounces.

Such considerations, along with the observation that reference often correlates rather with the receiver's interpretation than with the sender's expectations, and sometimes with neither, may have led one of the foremost proponents of the speech-act theory to drop or at least modify it drastically.[24] Notice, furthermore, that while we can by fiat let almost anything denote almost anything else, we cannot so easily let something represent or describe something else. The denotation effected will constitute representation or description only if what denotes belongs to and is functioning within a representational or descriptive system;[25] and to accomplish that requires something more than just a speech act.

Early in his paper, Kjørup writes of the two questions "What does this picture denote or refer to, if anything?" and "What kind of picture is this?" that they

differ fundamentally, belong to different realms of logic, so to speak. Only the latter may be said to be a strictly pictorial question, namely in the sense that it can be answered by way of an analysis of a given picture and a given pictorial system only, disregarding the non-pictorial context. The former, however, is of a more general sort, both in the sense that it may be raised and answered in exactly the same way about verbal utterances, say, as about pictorial ones, and in the sense that it has to be answered through a general analysis and understanding of the whole actual communicational situation.

This puzzles me. The question whether a picture is of a given kind and the question whether a description is of a given kind seem to me quite as parallel as are the questions what the picture

24. See John Searle's paper for the Cassirer celebration in Hamburg in October 1975, unpublished. The argument in my third from last paragraph above is much the same as one stressed by Searle.

25. The fiat would have to be: "Let p, functioning as a symbol in pictorial (or descriptive) system S, denote k". But if there is available no familiar pictorial (or descriptive) system in which p does denote k, one would have to provide a new system to serve as our S.

and the description denote. And "growling, barking, biting watchdog of Britain" is, on the face of it, quite as evidently a dog-description of Churchill as any picture could be a dog-picture of him.

While I have stressed the difference between representing a soandso and being a soandso-picture, I have also stressed their interrelation. My extensional theory treats both in terms of denotation: the one as a matter of what a picture denotes, the other as a matter of what denotes the picture. I find it odd that Kjørup does not likewise try to deal with both in terms of speech acts. Instead, when offering an explanation of what is involved in representing a soandso, he takes for granted the notion of being a soandso-picture. His condition *c* in Section 9, for example, begins:

The picture P counts as an R-representation in a pictorial language PL that the producer Pr knows and believes his audience A to know.

If he can accept what it is for a picture to count as an R-representation in a language that people know, without explaining in terms of acts or intents or beliefs how the picture came so to count in such a language, why then not equally placidly accept without explanation what it is for a picture to count as denoting a soandso in a known langauge?

Furthermore, the very idea of formulating reference in terms of the symbol-producer's belief makes me uncomfortable. How strong must the belief be? And how well justified? Is the belief, even if entirely wrong, enough? And why is the producer's belief taken as determining the reference even when the receiver may understand the symbol differently or not at all?

On the other hand, Kjørup perceives the importance of seeking a coordinated account of symbols that will cover pictorial as well as linguistic systems—of examining, for instance, what if any analog can be found in a pictorial system for the subject-predicate relation in language. And his effort to define the notion of *illustration* is original and interesting. I am sure he would not claim to have said the last word on this subject, but he has at least said some early ones.

*   *   *

Beginning with what seems a purely terminological dispute, Richard Martin ends with total rejection of most of the major theses of *Languages of Art* and *Ways of Worldmaking.*[26] He opposes using "denotation" to cover both verbal description (predication, naming) and pictorial representation, writing:

there is a long tradition that 'denotation' be taken more narrowly to stand for a relation only between word and object, and not between a nonlinguistic entity and an object. . . . The behavior of 'denotes' is subject to exact semantical rules just as 'truth' is. At this stage, it would seem unwise to run counter to such well-entrenched usage and rules.

Very well, use whatever words you like so long as you make clear how you are using them. But that will not satisfy him. He objects not merely to the use of "denotation" for a relation that embraces description and representation but to the very idea of such a generic relation and to the very idea of a still broader relation of reference or symbolization. In a passage amazing from one so devoted to formal systematization he writes:

it is not clear that the relations of representing, expressing, and exemplifying are *symbolic* relations in any strict sense. Rather they are *sui generis,* each having its own structure.

and later:

the work of art does not *stand for* [the relata of these relations] or "take the place of them". . . . To symbolize is to take the place of for some purpose or other. A painting does not take the place of whatever it represents, expresses, or exemplifies.

To work backward, how can a word "take the place of" a denoted nonverbal object? Neither within language, where the nonverbal object cannot have occurred, nor outside language, where the word as word does not occur, can the word replace the object. But that a portrait does *stand for* or refer to its subject and that any pictorial representation stands for or is a label for or refers to what it represents seems to me quite clear. The real

26. "On Some Aesthetic Relations", *Journal of Aesthetics and Art Criticism* 39 (1981) 275–277.

issue is not over terminology but over whether description, representation, etc. are all *sui generis*. To say that several relations are *sui generis* cannot mean that they do not have exactly the same structure; difference in structure does not preclude their having signficant common properties, or their logical sum from having important properties of its own. That relations are *sui generis* can only mean that their common properties and the properties of any more general relations including them are not signficant but are rather, in effect, misbegotten products of *ad hoc* couplings. I maintain that, on the contrary, description and representation have evident and important affinities, and that these relations together with exemplification and expression and many another relation have important properties common and peculiar to referential relations, where something does stand for, refer to, symbolize something else, or even itself.[27]

I am by no means suggesting that the specific differences between these relations be overlooked; rather, recognition of genera that embrace several relations invites examination of the differentia among the species, with the goal an organized basis for a general theory of symbols. Martin's denial that there are any nonverbal symbols and that the relations I call symbolic have anything important in common strikes me as a backward step in the understanding of the nature of the arts, the sciences, and language. Such a stance blocks, for example, the recognition that exemplification and expression are alike in running in the opposite direction from denotation, and that their difference from each other depends upon the difference between the literal and the metaphorical.

Incidentally, when Martin wants to speak generally of the relations I call referential, he calls them aesthetic relations. That is a highly inappropriate description since they are as common in nonaesthetic as in aesthetic contexts.[28]

27. I do not, as Martin implies in one place, "subsume [these] relations under denotation" but rather under the broader relation of reference. Exemplification and expression are *non*denotational but referential relations.

28. This holds even for exemplification, although it is a symptom of the aesthetic. See further IV,6 below.

Early in his discussion, Martin writes that exemplification involves no parameter for the painter or viewer, "exemplification being independent of such". But if which things a given label labels involves such a parameter, how can which labels label a given thing be independent of such? Furthermore, since which of the labels among those that label x are exemplified by x obviously varies with context and person, exemplification might be said to be doubly dependent thereon.

Later, an especially curious passage appears:

Nothing has been said thus far concerning the referential character of this relation. The various aesthetic relations here are not subsumed under reference or denotation, as with Goodman . . . To handle the referentiality of 'Exmpl' we need to consider another representation-relation, that between pictures and *properties* (or as here, predicates). This representation-relation is of course very different from that above, which is of objects or events. To handle this we may use (4) 'α Repr $_\rho\alpha$'.

In other words, exemplification, though not subsumed under reference, is subsumed under representation, so that depiction and expression are species of representation in general! But how can this abnormal use of "representation" be reconciled either with the little sermon, quoted above, on sticking to entrenched usage or with the dictum that each of the "aesthetic" relations be considered "on its own"? And if we are willing, as I am, to modify ordinary usage for technical purposes, still the grouping of depiction and exemplification under "representation" is surely unfortunate; for this obscures the difference in direction of reference between a relation that runs from label to labeled and another that runs from labeled to label (or correlated feature)— the difference between a relation R and another that is a subrelation of the converse of R.

In Martin's discussion of expression, two further faults appear. He supposes that expression is always of feelings or emotions possessed by the observer of a work; for example, by a person who "gains a feeling of grandeur . . . from a painting". In the first place, expression is not always of feelings or emotions; a black-and-white drawing may express motion, weight, or even color. In the second place, a feeling expressed by a work cannot be identified with the feeling aroused in the viewer; a painting expressing pain may arouse pity, a sculpture expressing ferocity may arouse fear, and a rhapsody expressing maudlin sentiment may arouse disgust. A feeling expressed by a work need not be experienced or literally possessed by the observer but must be metaphorically possessed by the work itself.

Martin remarks in closing that "we must lay the foundations for aesthetic analysis more firmly." Indeed.

6. STATEMENTS AND PICTURES

Although languages are obviously theory-laden, a language is on the face of it quite different from a theory stated in the language. A language makes no claims, is neutral as between opposing statements, accommodates varied and conflicting theories. A theory makes claims that can be denied in the same language and restated in other languages.

Thus Richard Rudner's argument to show that languages cannot be distinguished from theories startles us;[29] but it cannot be lightly dismissed. To understand a language is not merely to know what its terms are and how to put them together properly, but to know also what its terms mean or at least apply to. But if we know what "man" applies to and what "mortal" applies to, we already know that "all men are mortal" is true. The truth of the statement and the application of its terms are interdependent. To determine either is to determine the other and thus, the argument runs, languages and theories cannot be distinguished from each other.

Yet plainly in some sense we may know a language—as I know English—and still be in doubt about the truth of many statements in that language. Indeed, only if I in some sense understand a language can I set out to determine whether certain statements in it are true. How can we recognize such obvious facts without reviving the spurious distinction, long ago discred-

29. In "Show or Tell: Incoherence among Symbol Systems", *Erkenntnis* 12 (1978) 176–179.

ited by Quine, between the analytic and synthetic, between internal and external questions? Our trouble here, I think, lies in the nature of knowing a language. Knowing *all* about a language would include knowing the truth-value of every statement in it; but no one knows any language that way. As a matter of fact, knowing all about any one thing would amount to knowing all about everything; to know all about the fallen sparrow in Brooklyn is to know it fell just so many years, months, weeks, days, hours, minutes, seconds after a certain Chinese mandarin drank his ninety-second cup of tea in Soochow. But in any ordinary sense, knowing is partial, and by knowing a term we mean something much less than knowing everything that it applies to. I understand the term "green" in that I know of some things that they are green, and of others that they are not green, even though I do not know of still other things (because I have not seen them, nobody has told me, I cannot make the inference from other available information, or because they are borderline cases) whether they are green or not. I may even know a term without knowing anything it applies to if I know some of its extensional relationships to other terms I know. And I know a language if I know thus partially some of its terms. Knowing a language in this way does not imply knowing the truth-value of all statements in it; and so, quite within the bounds of extensionality, languages are distinguished from statements and theories.

I want, then, to keep languages and symbol systems distinct from terms and statements and other verbal and nonverbal symbols that make up these languages and systems. Likewise, I think of works of art not, as Rudner sometimes does, as symbol systems, but rather as symbols within systems.

Rudner's main concern, however, is with certain relationships, especially the relationship of contrast or conflict or incompatibility, between theories or more generally between versions, that may be in the same language or in different languages or in symbol systems that are not languages at all. This is an important and difficult matter, much in the forefront of my own current research.

Recently we have heard a good deal about theories that,

rather than being logically incompatible with each other, are 'incommensurable', so that logical relationships do not obtain between them or are at least indeterminable. "Incommensurable" has always seemed to me a rather inappropriate term; for incommensurable quantities are not incomparable. The radius and circumference of a circle are incommensurable, but their lengths in terms of a common unit can be compared within any desired degree of precision. I take it that the claimed disparity between theories, even in the same language, is wider than that. However that may be, when we take into account not only different theories, whether or not in the same language, but also versions and visions in symbol systems that are not languages and that admit of no statements or truth-values, we face disparities of quite a different order.

Rudner takes his cue from my suggestion that while a musical score is best construed as a denoting character like

"——followed by——followed by——" etc.

where the blanks are filled by descriptions of notes or chords, we might alternatively interpret it as a statement like

"In John Doe's Opus 83, ——is followed by ——, which is followed by——" etc.

So taken, the score has truth-value and stands to other scores in the usual sentential relationships of compatibility, conflict, consequence. Rudner proposes following the same course for all denotational symbols, and this covers a good deal of territory including depictions. A picture of Babe Ruth hitting a homer is taken as saying in effect that Babe Ruth hits a homer; so that such pictures are also treated as statements. This leaves nondenotational symbols—for instance, abstract paintings and music. Rudner points out that exemplification and expression, like denotation, are forms of reference, and suggests treating such works also as symbols that make statements about what is referred to.[30]

---

30. The reader of Rudner's paper must, by the way, watch for departures from the terminology of *Languages of Art*. For instance, I have used "referent" as

This is a considered and constructive proposal, worked out in some detail, but it raises a number of questions. In the first place, while the sentential correlate of a score seems more or less uniquely indicated, that is less clear even for a verbal description. We readily turn "Babe Ruth hitting a homer" into "Babe Ruth hits a homer"; but what do we do about "the wrecked, yellow, 200 h.p. John Doe automobile?" A number of candidates, such as "John Doe's yellow 200 h.p. automobile is wrecked" and "the wrecked yellow 200 h.p. automobile is John Doe's", seem to have equal claims. We are even worse off when we come to pictures. What does a picture of the Black Forest say? The trouble here is not merely that as with the verbal description there are alternative sentential correlates but that the picture, being in a syntactically undifferentiated symbol system, does not resolve into separate word-like elements that make up sentence-like sequences. Any correlation of picture with statement is thus much more remote and arbitrary.

Rudner does not overlook such questions or dismiss them lightly. His answer, as I understand it, is that each symbol or version in effect says that it refers to what it does in fact refer to. The automobile description thus says in effect "I (the string of words) denote the wrecked, yellow, 200 h.p. John Doe automobile"; the painting says "I depict the Black Forest"; and a spritely rondo says "I express spriteliness". Presumably, the automobile description would be true or right if and only if there is such an automobile. But what could constitute a false or wrong picture of the Black Forest? Under this criterion, whatever depicts the Black Forest counts as a true or right picture of it; for all the picture claims is that it does depict the Black Forest. A picture that does not depict the Black Forest does not claim to do so, and thus cannot be counted as a false or wrong picture of the Black Forest. To allow for wrong pictures, we would have to interpret a picture of the Black Forest as saying something more than that it depicts the Black Forest. But then we must ask "What more?"; we no

a general term for anything referred to, whether denoted, exemplified, or expressed, reserving "compliant" for what is denoted. Rudner uses "compliant" as I use "referent".

longer have a clear general principle for unique correlation of a statement with a picture.

These remarks by no means amount to comprehensive or conclusive criticism of Rudner's interesting work-in-progress, but they may suggest some of the reasons why, in approaching the same cluster of problems from much the same base, I have taken almost the opposite course (WW, VII). Rather than assimilating scores, descriptions, and pictures to statements, I treat them all as nondeclarative: a score, description, picture, diagram, etc. may refer in various ways, or be a referential symbol with empty reference, but does not state. This avoids the difficulties outlined above; but since nondeclarative versions have no truth-value, we must start from scratch in investigating the nature and standards of rightness and wrongness of such versions. Instead of appealing to truth, we must seek a more general notion of rightness that may sometimes subsume and sometimes compete with truth. That's tough.

Although, strictly speaking, pictures are not and do not make statements, many pictures—especially but not exclusively serial and moving pictures—do 'tell stories' (see IV, 1 & 2 below), and telling stories surely seems close to making statements. If a picture tells a story, why isn't it true or false?

An answer often given is that the picture and a text may tell the same story, and that the picture is true or false only indirectly, only in that the text is true or false. This is reasonable enough so long as we do not infer that 'telling the same story' implies that there is something called the story that is not itself a version but is embodied in various versions. For two texts to tell the same story is for them to be intertranslatable; and translation is well-known to be nonunique and highly variable. What must be preserved in translation depends on context and purpose; never is there total preservation. But what is involved in translation between a text, which is and makes a statement, and a picture, which does not?

A picture, like a predicate, may denote certain events (or in the case of fiction, be a soandso-label). When the predicates in a text denote those same events[31] (or are also soandso-labels), the picture and the text are to that extent intertranslatable; and the picture, though it makes no statement, might be derivatively called true or false according as the text is. But we must not forget that, strictly speaking, calling a picture true or false is false.

7. ABOUT TRUTH ABOUT

Things looked bad for Jones. His attorney, Lupoli, acknowledged that the testimony about Jones by Truman, chief witness for the prosecution, consisted of true statements, while the testimony about Jones by Falstaff, chief witness for the defense, consisted of false statements. Nevertheless, Lupoli claimed, none of the statements by Truman was true about Jones and none of the statements by Falstaff was false about him. The judge charged Lupoli with blatantly contradicting himself, threatened citation for contempt, and recessed court for the weekend.

Lupoli, noticing his client's dejected expression, took Jones aside and said, "I'll see you here—and at 9 A.M. sharp tomorrow." Jones protested, "But the court will be closed tomorrow." Lupoli replied, "I did not say I will see you here at 9 A.M. tomorrow. I said I will see you here (as I will on Monday) *and* will see you tomorrow at 9 A.M. (as I will in your cell). Seeing you at a given place and at a given time does not imply seeing you at that place at that time; so perhaps I can show the judge that a statement about you that is true may still not be true about you".

On Monday, Lupoli began his argument: "Your honor, all of us acknowledge you to be exceptionally able. You are also a golfer. But I leave it to you, thinking back over your scores this weekend, whether you are an exceptionally able golfer. The witnesses testified about Jones; Truman spoke truths, Falstaff spoke falsehoods. Nevertheless, Truman's testimony was not true about Jones, and Falstaff's testimony was not false about Jones".

If Jones committed no murder and gold is yellow, then

Jones committed murder or gold is yellow

though about Jones and true, is surely not true about Jones. On the other hand, the statement

31. Not that there is any unique criterion for considering two versions, verbal or pictorial, to denote the same events.

Jones committed no murder and gold is blue

though about Jones and false, is not false about Jones.

What we encounter here are instances of a more general phenomenon, characteristically overlooked by logicians, that might be called *consolidation*. It is not captured by mere conjunction, as is evident from such facts as that occurrence at a given place and at a given time does not imply occurrence at that place at that time, or that being skillful and a carpenter does not imply being a skillful carpenter.[32] The point penetrates acutely when one tries to articulate adequately the logical form of a sentence like

Smith is bad and a singer but not a bad singer.

Our concern at present, however, is not with the general matter of consolidation, but with the notion of *true about*. For two reasons little attention has been paid to that notion: first, the mistaken supposition, illustrated above, that *true about* is equivalent to the conjunction of *true* and *about*, when in fact that conjunction is neither a necessary nor a sufficient condition for *true about*; and, second, the failure to notice that *true about* serves in discourse an important purpose that is wrongly supposed to be served by the much weaker notion *true of*. An ordinary predicate or open sentence is normally *true of* certain things and not true of others, but a statement or closed sentence is true of everything if true of anything.[33] To say that a statement is true of Jones is just to say that the statement is true, whether it has anything to do with Jones or not. "Gold is yellow" is true of Jones in that Jones, like everything else, is such that gold is yellow. Since for statements "true of ——" means nothing other than "true", the no-

32. Perhaps related, if somewhat distantly, are problems raised in Anthony Kenny's book *Action, Emotion and Will* (London: Routledge & Kegan Paul, 1963) and studied further in Romane Clark's "Concerning the Logic of Predicate Modifiers," *Noûs*, 4 (1970) 311–335, and Donald Davidson's "The Logical Form of Action Sentences," in Nicholas Rescher, ed., *The Logic of Decision and Action* (Pittsburgh: Pittsburgh University Press, 1966), pp. 81–120.

33. This is just the degenerate case of the semantic commonplace that a formalized sentence with at most one free variable is true of (or false of) an object if an only if uniform supplantation of that free variable by a name of the object yields a truth (or a falsehood).

tion of a statement's being true of something is superfluous and may as well be dropped in favor of the notion of the statement's being true.[34] On the other hand, not all true statements are *true about* Jones, and not all statements true about Jones are true.[35]

Once we are clear that *true about* is not merely *true of* or *true* and is not the conjunction of *true* and *about*, we enter upon a rather intricate problem of analysis. Some sample cases are quite clear; others call for difficult decisions. We will understand "about" in the sense of *absolutely about*, as it was explicated in "About" (*PP*, VI). A statement *S* counts as *about k* if and only if *S* has a consequence *T* that contains an expression designating *k* while *S* implies no generalization of *T* with respect to any part of that designating expression. For the present we confine our attention to designating expressions that would be formalized as constants, as opposed both to compound terms and to predicates. With this restriction we can avail ourselves of an especially crisp formulation: *S* is about *k* if and only if *S* does not imply its own generalization with respect to some name of *k*; for example, "ϕk" is about *k* if "ϕk" does not imply "$(x)\phi x$".[36]

Now consider a disjunction with a true and a false component:

(1) Vermont is a state or Boston is a state

which is about Vermont, about Boston, and true—and clearly also true about Vermont. But it is pretty clearly *not* true about Boston. How so? A naive answer might be that (1) consists of two component statements such that only one is about Boston and that one is not true. But this will not do as a general principle; for (1) is logically equivalent to "If Boston is not a state then Vermont is a state", in which all components that are about Boston

34. Superfluous for such practical purposes as ours, that is. Analogs of "true of", even for closed sentences, play crucial roles in the standard Tarski truth definition.

35. "A true statement about Jones" seems to be ambiguous as between "a statement both true and about Jones" and "a statement true about Jones".

36. The assumption here is that "ϕk" contain "k" wherever "ϕx" has free "x"—in short, that it be an instance of "$(x)\phi x$".

are true. Logically equivalent statements can hardly be such that one is true about something that the other is not true about.

A better suggestion, perhaps, is that (1) is not true about Boston because in one important way (1) does not differentiate between Boston and anything else: no matter what name we put in place of "Boston" in (1), the resulting disjunction is still true. On the other hand, (1) does thus differentiate Vermont from some other things; for the result of replacing "Vermont" in (1) by, say, "Toronto" will be a false statement. This provisional explanation of why (1) is true about Vermont but not true about Boston parallels the analysis of "about", but with truth supplanting implication. For example, "Everything is boring and so is *Emma*" is not even about *Emma*; for a statement is not about *k* if it implies with respect to each thing what it purports to say about *k*. In considering what (1) is true about, however, what matters is not the implication but the *truth* of results of replacing "Boston" by other names. This is not surprising; for although truth of a statement is not requisite for its truth about something, truth quite naturally plays a role in the explication of *true about* that it does not play in the explication of *about*.

If (1) is thus true about Vermont but not true about Boston, is (1) thereby false about Boston? We cannot very well condemn (1) as a lie about Boston; for, since Vermont is a state, (1) makes no commitment about Boston and so tells no falsehood about it. Thus it appears that even among statements about *k* some are neither *true about k* nor *false about k* but merely *twaddle about k*. Twaddle about *k* may be true or false.

Next, consider a conjunction having a true and a false component:

(2) Vermont is not a state and Boston is not a state

which is about Vermont, about Boston, and false. Pretty clearly, (2) is false about Vermont. Like (1), it differentiates between Vermont and some other things; replacement of "Vermont" by "Toronto" in (2) will change the truth-value of the whole—this time from false to true. This was to be expected, since (2) is equivalent to (1)'s negation. And as (1), though true, is not true about Boston, so (2), though false, is not false about Boston. Like (1), (2) does not differentiate in the specified way between Boston and anything else. But here the parallel ends; for, since a conjunction, unlike a disjunction, is committed to each one of its components, (2) is not merely not false about Boston but makes a true commitment about Boston—is, in short, true about Boston. Our tentative differentiation criterion does not cover this case.

In summary so far: (1) is true about Vermont but neither true about nor false about Boston; (2) is false about Vermont and true about Boston. These initial cases have to some extent challenged intuition and resisted our first attempts at uniform explanation. Before going further, we may well survey some minimal conditions of adequacy for a definition of *true about*. We have already implicitly demanded that a statement count as true about *k* or false about *k* only if it is about *k*; and that any equivalent of a statement true about (or false about) *k* be likewise true about (or false about) *k*. We can reasonably insist further that a statement and its negation cannot both be true about *k*, nor both false about *k*. And clearly also, no statement can be both true about *and* false about the same thing. But we had better stop there for now, avoiding such pitfalls as insisting that if a statement is true about *k* then its negation is false about *k*. For we have seen that although (2) is true about Boston, its negation (1) seems not to be false about Boston.[37]

So far we have considered (1), a disjunction of a truth and a falsehood, and (2), a conjunction of a truth and a falsehood. A disjunction of falsehoods, such as

(3) Vermont is not a state or Boston is a state

---

37. Carl Wellman has pointed out to us that a consequence (such as 3) of a statement true about Boston (such as 2) may be false about Boston. This notable fact is not unparalleled; for a consequence of a statement about Boston may not be about Boston. Only such consequences of a statement about Boston as follow differentially with respect to Boston are sure to be about Boston. Similarly, at most those consequences of a statement true about Boston that follow differentially with respect to Boston are sure to be true about Boston. Further investigation is needed to determine whether additional reservations are needed for more complex cases.

offers no difficulty. It is plainly false about Vermont and false about Boston; and it does differentiate each of them from other things in the way specified, since replacement of either "Vermont" or "Boston" by another name may result in a true disjunction. A conjunction of truths is equally unproblematic:

(4) Vermont is a state and Boston is not a state

is clearly true about, and differentiates, both Vermont and Boston.

Trouble returns, however, when we come to a conjunction of falsehoods such as

(5) Vermont is not a state and Boston is a state

which though surely false about both Vermont and Boston seems not to differentiate either one; for no replacement of either "Vermont" or "Boston" alone is sufficient to yield a true statement. The conjunction tells two lies, but our faltering differentiation criterion would leave it as not false about either Vermont or Boston. A disjunction of truths raises much the same problem:

(6) Vermont is a state or Boston is not a state

is true about Vermont and Boston, yet appears to differentiate neither one.

Cases like (2), (5), and (6) confront us with the task of reconciling our general formula with some of our particular judgments.[38] That is harder than it may look.

The idea underlying our tentative differentiation criterion was that a statement is true about k or false about k if and only if it is about k and its truth-value rests upon k in that replacement of a name for k in the statement may change that truth-value. This, however, mistakenly fails to make (2) true about Boston, to make (5) false about Boston or false about Vermont, or to make (6) true about either. Now since the truth-value of any of these three statements may indeed be changed by replacing *both* "Vermont" and "Boston" simultaneously, the truth-value might be said to rest upon Vermont and Boston jointly in these cases. But we

38. This is another instance of a familiar problem. See *FFF*, pp. 63 ff.

must proceed cautiously. For to take resting jointly on k and some l as a sufficient condition for truth about k or falsity about k would err in the opposite direction, wrongly making (1), for example, true about Boston. We need a subtler criterion, free of both faults.

This will give some idea of the nature and difficulty of the search for adequate definitions of "true about", "false about", and "twaddle about". The rest of that search need not be recounted here;[39] but the definitions adopted as well as those needed along the way will be found in the technical appendix below, and some consequences of those definitions may now be outlined.

Notice that unlike "false", which for statements is the complement of "true", "false about" is not the complement of "true about" but only one of three subdivisions of that complement. A statement not true about k may be either (i) not about k at all, (ii) about k but not false about k, and so twaddle, or (iii) false about k. In the practical cases that exercise and develop our intuitions, what concerns us seems most often to be whether a statement is or is not true about a given subject, rather than how a statement not true about the subject is more specifically classified.

Furthermore, statements false about k must be false, while those true about k may have either truth-value. This is just the reflection of how conjunction works; for true conjuncts may belong either to true or to false conjunctions, while false conjuncts belong only to false conjunctions.

Twaddle about k, though neither true about k nor false about k, may itself be either true or false.

In the table below we assume that *"Pa"*, *"Ta"*, and *"Tb"* are all true while *"Fa"*, *"Fb"*, *"Ga"*, and *"Gb"* are all false. For simplicity we assume that the predicates are mutually independent, in that no consistent Boolean combination of them has empty extension. We tabulate twelve cases, putting *"tr"*, *"fs"*, and

39. A detailed report can be found in "Truth About Jones", *Journal of Philosophy* 74 (1977) 317–338, by Joseph Ullian and Nelson Goodman. The present section is an abridgment of that paper.

"TW" for "true about", "false about", and "twaddle about", respectively:

Statement	Truth-value	Status
#1 Pa · Ta	True	tr a
#2 Pa · Tb	True	tr a, tr b
#3 Pa · Fa	False	fs a
#4 Pa · Fb	False	tr a, fs b
#5 Fa · Ga	False	fs a
#6 Fa · Gb	False	fs a, fs b
#7 Pa ∨ Ta	True	tr a
#8 Pa ∨ Tb	True	tr a, tr b
#9 Pa ∨ Fa	True	tr a
#10 Pa ∨ Fb	True	tr a, TW b
#11 Fa ∨ Ga	False	fs a
#12 Fa ∨ Gb	False	fs a, fs b

#4 is false and about a yet true about a. #10 is true and about b but not true about b; nor is it false about b either. No wonder we have taken pains to avoid such phrases as "a truth about k" and "a true statement about k"; the ambiguity they threaten is serious.

Full coverage for more complex statements, composed of many clauses or containing quantifiers or ostensibly speaking of unicorns or Pickwick, is enormously difficult.[40] But perhaps enough has been said here to show that for more reasons than one, even rather simple truth about Jones is often hard to find.

TECHNICAL APPENDIX

Formulae proposed and discussed in "Truth about Jones":
A *minimal set* for a sentence consists of names all of which must be replaced to change the truth-value of the sentence. (Plainly, a sentence can have more than one minimal set.)

---

40. First thoughts on some of these matters are noted in the "Postscript" (pp. 334–338) to "Truth About Jones", cited in note 39 above.

A *regular* equivalent of a sentence is a nonredundant equivalent in conjunctive normal form.

S strongly depends on k if and only if k is named by a member of one of S's minimal sets.

S depends on k if and only if every regular equivalent of S contains conjuncts whose conjunction strongly depends on k.

S is true about k if and only if S depends on k and there is a regular equivalent of S in which every conjunct that is about k contains a true disjunct that is about k.

S is false about k if and only if S depends on k and there is a regular equivalent of S in which some conjunct that is about k is false.

S is twaddle about k if and only if S is about k but neither true about k nor false about k.

IV. Art in Theory

Since in my view the arts and the sciences are alike means of understanding, using symbol systems of various kinds, we have often encountered the arts in the preceding chapters. But the following discussions are somewhat more specifically or predominantly concerned with the arts, or find in the arts primary examples of more general theory.

The first question considered is how narrative is distinguished from other types of discourse. Twisting the order of events in the telling can go far, but not beyond certain limits, without loss of story. But "The Telling and the Told" reminds us that the twisting in the telling is always relative not to an absolute order of occurrence but to the *told* order. Some questions concerning style are then discussed. A review of the status of symptoms of the aesthetic and the rationale for their selection leads to "Virtue Confined", which began with correcting a misreading of passages from *Languages of Art* but has now been revised and expanded to combat prevalent mistaken identification of the aesthetic with the aesthetically excellent.

"On the Identity of Works of Art" clarifies the concepts of autographic and allographic arts and the way that dependence upon history of production distinguishes between them. And it suggests the need for some further work relating these matters to current debates among theorists of literature on questions concerning correctness of interpretation.

Reflections on the role of implementation in the arts point toward Chapter V.

1. TWISTED TALES

OR, STORY, STUDY, AND SYMPHONY

The eighth race at Rockingham the other day was reported in the newspaper as follows:

Excalibur broke last from the gate, took the lead by the far turn, then dropped back to fourth coming into the stretch, but rallied to win by a nose.

My own report that evening to a friend who had bet on Excalibur went:

Excalibur won by a nose, though he was fourth coming into the stretch after leading at the far turn despite having broken last from the gate.

Nothing strikes us as unusual here even though the order of telling completely reverses the order of occurrence. Indeed, to have withheld the result of the race to the end would have been inconsiderate under the circumstances. In other reports the telling may jump back and forth; for example:

Excalibur, though he broke last from the gate, won by a nose after having dropped back to fourth, coming into the stretch, from the lead he had taken by the far turn.

or

Excalibur won by a nose although, after breaking last from the gate and taking the lead at the far turn, he had dropped back to fourth coming into the stretch.

And the twenty other sequences of telling are equally admissible.

A series of snapshots taken at the four stages of the race in question and showing enough of the surroundings would, presented in any order, tell the same story. Even without such helpful verbal devices as tenses and words like "before" and "then", the order of occurrence can be readily determined. Again, a film of the race can be cut and spliced to conform to any of the different orderings possible in a verbal report. Cinema and literature alike would be severely handicapped if required always to report incidents in the order of their occurrence.

In sum, flashbacks and foreflashes are commonplace in narrative, and such rearrangements in the telling of a story seem to leave us not only with a story but with very much the same story.[1] In the reports of the race, for example, no time twisting will leave us without a story or with an altogether different story. But is this true in general? Will no disparity between the order of telling and the order of occurrence destroy either the basic identity or the narrative status of any story? An exception seems ready at hand: suppose we simply run our film of the race backward. The result, though a story, seems not to be the same story in any usual sense but rather to be a story of the horse running *backward* from finish line to starting gate. Does cinematic narrative actually differ this sharply from narrative in a series of snapshots or in words? I think not. Our first impulse with any tale when the order of telling is clear is to take the order of occurrence to be the same as the order of telling; we then make any needed corrections in accord with temporal indications given in the narrative and with our antecedent knowledge both of what happened and of causal processes in general. But discrepancy between order of telling and order of occurrence cannot always be discovered instantaneously—or at all. If our series of snapshots is shown in reverse order at normal speed, we readily detect the reversal; for we know that a race begins at the starting gate, ends at the finish line, and so on. Even if the pictures do not show the starting gate or finish line or other identifiable parts of the track, we are not deceived; for we know that horses do not run backward. But when the *film* is run backward, such clues and considerations usually cannot be brought to bear soon enough, and we momentarily mistake the direction of the actions filmed. A little time is needed to make the correction. What seemed like a drastic difference between film and other forms of narrative amounts to nothing more than this lag.

Suppose, though, our film is of an automobile moving slowly

1. In an obvious and important sense. Of course, whether two versions are properly said to be of the same story—or of the same world—depends upon which of many permissible interpretations of sameness is understood; but that need not trouble us here.

along an otherwise empty street. Since automobiles can go forward or backward, I cannot tell whether I am seeing a film run backward of an automobile going forward or a film run forward of an automobile going backward. Such ambiguity is not an exclusive property of film either. A series of snapshots of the automobile would be equally ambiguous; so also would a narrative in words where neither verbal indications nor knowledge of the particular event or of causal process determines order of occurrence. In all these cases, the order of occurrence is indeterminate and remains so under any transformation of the order of telling.

In other cases, the order of occurrence is determinate but vacuous. *The Conversion of Saint Paul* by Pieter Bruegel (Kunsthistorische Museum, Vienna) tells a story and tells it so compellingly that we tend to forget that nothing in the picture literally moves, that no part of the picture precedes any other in time, and that what is explicitly shown is not actions taking place but a momentary state. Neither the telling nor what is explicitly told takes time; the picture is a timeless tale, without sequence of occurrence and also without sequence of telling; for there is no one mandatory or even preferred order of reading the picture—of translating its spatial relationships into temporal ones. And since the order of telling and the order of occurrence are both vacuous, no question arises of varying the relationship between the two. Reversing the picture reverses the spatial relationships in both picture and pictured but has no temporal effect.

Implicitly, of course, such a picture as the Bruegel tells a story of events before and after—and inferred from—the state explicitly depicted. What is thus implicitly told takes time, though its telling does not. The vacuous order of telling differs drastically from the order of occurrence but is still invariable.

Jacopo del Sellaio tells the story of Psyche in quite another way (Museum of Fine Arts, Boston). Here what is explicitly told takes time, and the telling has a definite order. Several incidents, with Psyche appearing in each, are shown strung across a landscape. The impossibility of the same person's being in different places at the same time notifies us that difference in spatial position among scenes is to be interpreted as difference in temporal position among the events depicted. And, as with a written tale, although the whole story is presented at once, an order of telling is plainly established. The main sequence here conforms to linguistic convention. In the West, pictorial narratives including comic strips tend to go from left to right; in the East, from right to left. This is clear when pictures of a series are on successive pages of a book or on a hand scroll, where the order of telling is plainly established. In many other cases, the influence of linguistic connection on pictorial narrative is weak and easily overruled. In the Sellaio, the main direction of telling is fixed by the orientation of the larger figures of Psyche: five of the eight face right, and two of these, moreover, slant to the right; a sixth shows Psyche lying prone with head to the right; only one, near the right end, faces left—for the sake of design. Two slight deviations from left-to-right sequence of telling occur: in the background at the left is a sort of prologue with Psyche and companions facing left; and in the center, Psyche is shown as standing, with head turned back, at the bottom of a path that winds upward and directs attention to the next scene, at the top of the path and just left of the preceding lower scene. How much more the orientation of the figures counts for in effecting the order of telling in this picture can be seen by simply reversing the whole picture, which then reads the opposite way.

Where the order of telling is evident but the order of occurrence is not known and cannot be inferred, we sometimes assume that the order of occurrence follows the order of telling; but even when we happen to be right, as in the case of the Sellaio, our guess is groundless. Nothing dictates agreement between the two orders. The painter might have chosen to flash forward to depict the last incident first, at the left end of the picture; or he might, keeping the orientation of each scene unchanged, have reversed their order completely, thus telling his story backward. Altogether different is the result of reversing the picture as a whole: the telling is then from right to left, but the match between order of telling and order of occurrence is unaffected, so that the story is still told not backward but from beginning to end.

In Piero di Cosimo's *Discovery of Honey* (Fogg Art Museum,

Cambridge, Mass.), which depicts three incidents in the legend of Silenus, what is told takes time but the order of telling is unclear.[2] If we take it to be from left to right, we have an example of foreflash; for in order of occurrence, the incident depicted in the center (Silenus falling off his mount) comes first, that at the right (the attempt to lift him onto his feet) second, and that at the left (boys rubbing mud on his stings) last. From left to right the order of occurrence is thus 3, 1, 2—the last event being shown first. But direction of telling can no more be inferred from order of occurrence than conversely; and the direction of telling in this picture is not unmistakably from left to right. The scenes are not on a level line or on the same pictured plane and, what matters more, there are no such indications as the repeated left-right orientation of scenes in the Sellaio. Even thus lacking direction, though, the spatial arrangement of telling departs from the order of occurrence in that an event that does not occur between two others is depicted between them. Thus we have not a mere foreflash or flashback but a flashbetween.

More often than not, no time order of telling is indicated in a picture; but the spatial distribution of the incidents depicted often varies in many and remarkable ways in relation to the order of occurrence. In a painting of the legend of Marsyas,[3] from Pompeii, any indications of a sequence of telling are negligible. In order of occurrence, the scenes begin at the upper left and proceed counterclockwise to the upper right. In Ghiberti's bronze *Gates of Paradise*, the east doors of the Baptistry in Florence, the sequence of occurrence is from left to right in each line and from each line to the next below it; but in the same sculptor's earlier north doors, the sequence, though also from left to right in each line, is from each line to the next above it— perhaps for the convenience of observers standing on the ground. But here again we must be careful not to assume that

2. For help in finding many of my examples of pictorial narrative, I am grateful to Sydney Freedberg, George Hanfmann, Marianne Martin, Ann Milstein, and John Rosenfield.

3. See Christopher M. Dawson's *Romano-Companian Mythological Landscape Painting*, Yale Classical Studies, vol. 9 (New Haven: Yale University Press, 1944), p. 90.

this is also the order of telling, which—where there is one—must be determinable quite independently of order of occurrence.

Incidentally, even in the east doors the scenes within some individual panels are arranged otherwise than from left to right. For example, in the panel of *The Garden of Eden* at the upper left corner, although the three larger scenes are arranged left to right in order of occurrence, the Temptation is reduced in size and shoved into the background at the left rather than being placed between the center and right-hand scenes.

Memling's *Life of Christ* (Pinacoteca, Turin), like the Sellaio, depicts many incidents in a single landscape but provides little indication—by consistent orientation or winding paths or other means—of any order of telling. In order of occurrence the scenes follow a tortuous course from upper left to upper right (Figure 5), but nothing in the picture looked at apart from the subject makes this evident. The arrangement is two-dimensional (virtually even three-dimensional) without beginning or end or marked route. This pictorial organization of events of a lifetime is spatial, atemporal, motivated perhaps both by considerations of design

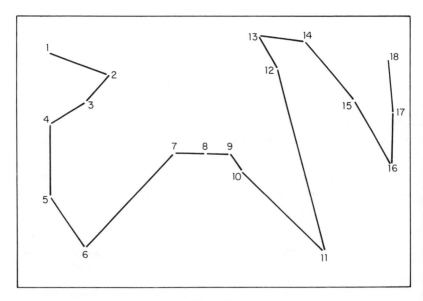

Figure 5.

and by regarding these events as eternal and emblematic rather than as episodic or transient.

In pictures like these, foreflashes and flashbacks and even flashbetweens, which are all departures in the telling from the sequence of occurrence, are out of the question; for here there is not only no direction but no order of telling at all. Rearranging scenes can result merely in different patterns being marked out by the sequence of occurrence. For example, if the first two scenes in the Pompeian picture are interchanged, the pattern will

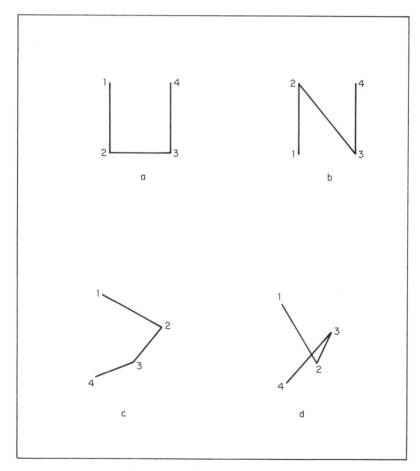

Figure 6. Diagram of effect of interchanges of scenes.

be as in Figure 6b rather than as in 6a, but neither constitutes order of telling. Interchanging the second and third scenes in the Memling gives the pattern in 6d rather than that in 6c. In such cases we have no different orders of telling or different degrees of deviation from order of occurrence but only different spatial patterns and, at most, different degrees of convolution relative to order of occurrence.

Even more complex than the organization of the Memling is that of a much older work: a 'picture biography' of the Japanese Buddhist Prince Shōtoku Taishi (Tokyo National Museum), painted by Hata no Chitei in 1069.[4] It consists of five large screens, making up one continuous picture, for hanging on three walls in the Hōryū-ji Temple. The landscape setting is Nara and the surrounding country; some of the buildings shown still survive and others are identifiable by documents. At the left end, across the water, is China. Against this background are some sixty scenes from the prince's life—or lives.

That the order of telling proceeds from right to left here is pretty definitely established by the Oriental convention, reinforced (as nearly as can be judged from available reproductions of the damaged paintings) by such internal indications as the way most figures and scenes face. But this differs drastically from the order of occurrence. Scenes from all periods of the prince's career appear on each screen: on the first screen the incidents date from conception to age twenty-seven; on the second, from age six to forty-three; on the third, from seventeen to forty-nine; on the fourth, from sixteen to fifty, when Shōtoku died; and on the right half of the fifth, from nine to thirty-seven. Furthermore, the scenes on each screen are not arranged in any simple chronological order, as may be seen from the diagrams in Figures 7 and 8; and were we to number the scenes consecutively over the whole series and connect each next pair with a line, the resulting diagram would be a terrible tangle. At the end—on the left side of the leftmost screen (Figure 9)—are scenes from the prince's

4. For much information concerning this work, I am grateful to John Rosenfield and to Aya Louisa McDonald, who has made available to me the results of her intensive but as yet unpublished study of it.

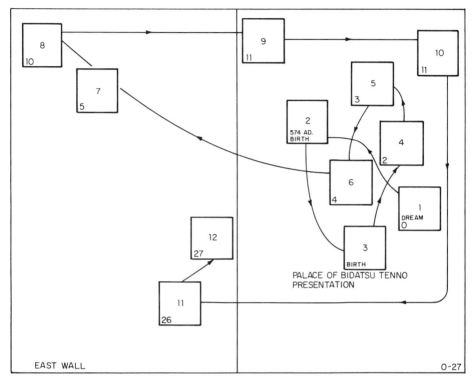

Figure 7. Plan of first screen of the series. The number in the lower left corner of each square stands for the prince's age at the time of the incident depicted. The number in the center of each square indicates the chronological position of the incident relative to the others depicted on this same screen.

previous incarnations. Here is a notable and venerable example of flashback—of earlier events being told later.

What principles govern this arrangement? The disadvantages of keeping to the chronological order and thus, for example, putting all childhood scenes on the first screen are obvious. Considerations of design combined with spiritual detachment from the temporal override any concern for chronological order. It has been suggested that the disposition of scenes in these paintings may be according to the place where the event occurred; for example, some of the first scenes show the prince being conceived in one room, born in another, and playing in the backyard. In the flashback, incidents from the prince's earlier incarnations are de-

117

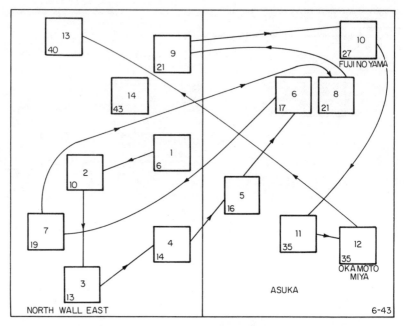

Figure 8. Plan of second screen of the same series.

picted as in China—'out of the country', apparently signifying 'out of this life'.

On this account, the organization is geographical rather than chronological, so that scene x appears to the right of scene y not because incident x occurred before but because it occurred east of incident y.[5] If so, the paintings constitute as much a map as a story of the prince's career. We do find maps—for example, a National Geographical Society pictorial map of England and Wales—with historical events depicted and even labeled at the map positions in question.[6] But the idea that the arrangement of scenes in the Shōtoku paintings is geographical seems on the face of it highly implausible. Could the events in the prince's life have been so happily distributed over the landscape? Indeed, examination shows conclusively that the arrangement in the paint-

5. Curiously, although Oriental texts read from right to left, the opposite way from ours, Oriental maps normally, I am told, have the west at the left and the east at the right just as ours do, the territory being mapped as if seen from the south of it.

6. But the Shōtoku paintings differ from such maps in having a well-established, and contrasting, right-to-left overall order of telling.

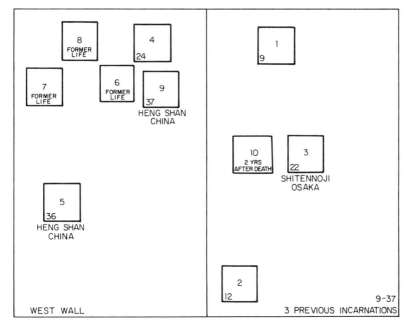

Figure 9. Plan of final screen of the series.

ings is not geographical in any usual sense; for example, pictures of a temple at different stages of completion are in different places, and there are two separate pictures of the prince's birth. Relative geographical position cannot be inferred from relative pictorial position according to any consistent plan. Furthermore, in another series of paintings of the prince's life, pictures of the same events are arranged in a quite different way.

If there is some factor at work here other than an unworldly and atemporal or even antitemporal outlook along with a concern for all aspects of design, I have yet to discover it; but that, after all, is the business of scholars in the field.

These varied verbal and pictorial examples show that in a narrative neither the telling nor what is explicitly told need take time, and they suggest furthermore that narrative reordered in any way at all is still narrative. That poses a problem, for although we think of narrative as the peculiarly temporal species of discourse, distinguished from description or exposition through meeting some time condition or other, we have so far discovered no such condition. That what is implicitly or explicitly told must take time hardly distinguishes narrative, for even description or depiction of a momentary and static situation implies something of what went before and will come afterward. A picture of a forest tells implicitly of trees growing from seedlings and shedding leaves; and a picture of a house implies that trees were cut for it and that its roof will soon leak.

How has the distinguishing feature of narrative escaped us? Perhaps by our concluding too hastily from the evidence considered that narrative under any transformation whatsoever of the order of telling is always still narrative. Actually, although every narrative will survive some reordering, and some narratives will survive any reordering, not every narrative will survive every reordering. Some stories when reordered in certain ways are no longer stories but studies. Consider, for example, a psychologist's report that recounts a patient's behavior chronologically. It is a story, a history. But rearranged to group the incidents according to their significance as symptoms—of, say, first suicidal tendencies, then claustrophobia, then psychopathic disregard of consequences—it is no longer a story but an analysis, a case study. Reordering of the telling here turns a narrative into something else.

Literature provides many a more notable example. Aldous Huxley's brilliant short piece on the abominable British painter Benjamin Robert Haydon contains enough reports of events in Haydon's life from childhood to death to constitute a brief biography;[7] but the arrangement of these reports is strikingly at variance with chronology. Incidents from several widely spaced periods of Haydon's life are often reported in a single paragraph. His suicide is mentioned in the middle of the paper, followed by descriptions of his marital and family life (including the straight-faced statement that one stepson "had a promising career in the navy cut short, in the Indian Ocean, by the bite of a sea-serpent"). An account of Haydon's late work and disappointments is followed by mention of the early mistake that led to his study of art. Now displacements in order of telling, as we have seen,

7. See Aldous Huxley's "B. R. Haydon," *The Olive Tree* (London: Chatto & Windus, 1936), pp. 239–261.

are not in general incompatible with narrative; but here, rather than heightening the story, they work against it, being guided by how the reported incidents document and illuminate various aspects of Haydon's character, among them vanity, self-dramatization, snobbery, romanticism, dishonesty, piety, literary skill, and wit. The result is no biography but a character study, no story but an essay on self-deception and other matters. The order of the telling so groups incidents reported as to bring out kinships and contrasts that cut across and obliterate—or at least blur—the story line. Narrative gives way to exposition.

While I have at hand no actual pictorial example where the organization of scenes according to themes or characteristics makes it a study rather than a story, such a picture could easily be produced. Scenes from the life of a saint, for instance, might be grouped into those of temptations resisted, persecutions suffered, miracles performed, and so on, so that the chronicle would be dispersed and denatured under a classification of events into religiously significant kinds.

The classification that supersedes or subordinates chronology is not always in terms of topical features. Sometimes, rather, it is in terms of expressive or other aesthetically relevant qualities, as in a theater piece that organizes its version of incidents in a hockey game, on the basis of dynamic and rhythmic properties, into movements like those of a musical work (III,2 above). In such cases, a story becomes more a symphony than a study.

In all these examples, what nullifies narrative is not the order of telling itself but the resultant alignment with certain categories that are—or are to be made—highly relevant in the context and for the purpose at hand. World structure is heavily dependent on order of elements and on comparative weight of kinds; and reordering and weight-shifting are among the most powerful processes used in making and remaking facts and worlds. Although in the psychologist's report and the Huxley, the status as study rather than story is reinforced by interspersed discursive passages, the reorganization alone would, I think, suffice. So also would a reordering that emphasizes significant features otherwise than by a simple sorting of incidents. In other cases, narrative status rather than being nullified is merely subdued. And where order of occurrence itself happens to yield a sorting into prominent categories, we may have what is both a story and a study or symphony. These types of discourse, though distinct, are not mutually exclusive.

The general lesson, then, is that while narrative will normally survive all sorts of contortion, still sometimes when we start with a tale, enough twisting may leave us without one.

2. THE TELLING AND THE TOLD

In the course of her "Narrative Versions, Narrative Theories",[8] Barbara Herrnstein Smith seems to intimate that my "Twisted Tales" is incompatible with what I have urged in *Ways of World-making* and other writings. To clear away any misunderstanding, let me show that nothing in my paper makes any concession to absolutism, 'dualism', or 'deep structure'.

In distinguishing between order of telling and order of occurrence, I am not supposing that order of occurrence is an absolute order of events independent of all versions but am rather drawing the distinction between order of the telling and order of the *told*. Consider some brief tales:

1. Lincoln's assassination preceded Kennedy's.
2. Kennedy's assassination followed Lincoln's.

In (1) the orders of the telling and the told agree. In (2), on the other hand, the order of telling reverses the order of the told, and we have a twisted tale. But the twisting is with respect not to an order of events apart from all versions but to what this version *says* is the order of events.

The distinction between order of the telling and order of the told holds for false as well as for true tales. For instance:

3. Kennedy's assassination preceded Lincoln's.
4. Lincoln's assassination followed Kennedy's.

8. *Critical Inquiry* 7 (1980) 213-236.

In (3) the orders of the telling and the told agree, while in (4) the order of telling reverses the order of the told. Although both (3) and (4) are false, (4) is twisted while (3) is not.

The tales may even be entirely fictional:

5. Washington's assassination preceded Truman's.
6. Washington's assassination followed Truman's.

The orders of the telling and the told agree in (5) but differ in (6).

Thus the distinction between order of the telling and order of the told does not imply truth, or that events told of occurred in a given order, or even that there are any such events. This holds equally well where the order of the told is implicit or inferential rather than explicit. Consider the following tale of Don Quixote:

7. The windmill won. He returned covered with mud.

In this tale, the two orders agree; but interchanging the sentences gives a twisted tale. In other cases, such as (3) and (6), what might otherwise be the implicitly told order is overruled by an explicitly told order.

All this would have been clearer had I written *"told* order of occurrence" rather than simply "order of occurrence" in my paper. Still, fictional examples like the Jacopo del Sellaio and the Piero di Cosimo paintings are plain evidence of what I meant.

One further point: if I say that the geocentric and the heliocentric systems describe the same motion, I do not imply that there is some absolute motion that both systems describe but only that the two systems are related in a certain way. If I say that two terms have the same or virtually the same meaning, I am not saying that there is any such entity as a meaning that they have but am only speaking of a relation between the terms. And when I speak of several versions of the same or virtually the same story, I am by no means conceding that there is some underlying story, some deep structure, that is not itself a version.

3. FICTION FOR FIVE FINGERS

I submit the following theses: (1) All fiction is literal, literary falsehood. (2) Yet some fiction is true. (3) Truth of fiction has nothing to do with realism. (4) There are no fictive worlds. (5) Not all literal, literary falsehood is fiction.

All fiction is literal, literary falsehood.

Literal falsity distinguishes fiction from true report; but falsity alone does not make fiction. 'Plain lies, damn lies, and statistics' are not fiction; neither are mistakes, whether computer or human, whether misprints, miscalculations, or misconceptions. Only literary falsehood is fiction. That no more implies that all fiction has literary merit than to say that the pictures in an exhibition are works of art implies that all are good. What constitutes art, literary or otherwise, is not a question to be settled here. I have suggested elsewhere (IV,6 below) certain features that are symptomatic of art; and perhaps the most prominent of these for literature are the use of exemplification and expression, and of multiple and complex reference. With the scientific text or book of instructions, what matters most is what is said; for the literary work, forms and feelings and other features exemplified or expressed or signified through varied short or long referential chains usually count for more.

Yet some fiction is true.

Although all fiction is literally false, some is metaphorically true. And while metaphorical truth is compatible with literal falsity, metaphorical truth contrasts with metaphorical falsity quite as cleanly as does literal truth with literal falsity (*LA*, pp. 68–71). In other words, a term with a literal range of application—that is, a literal extension—often has another, metaphorical extension. The two extensions may, but need not, be quite separate. Most terms, indeed, are ambiguous both literally and metaphorically, having several different literal and several different metaphorical extensions; but that does not obscure the distinction between literal and metaphorical truth. The sound of thunder is not literally, but is metaphorically, a lion's roar.

Truth of fiction has nothing to do with realism.

What constitutes truth of a work, fiction or not, is a notoriously difficult question. But we need not answer it to see that truth of description, literal or metaphorical, like correctness of depiction, is independent of realism. For while truth or correctness depends upon what is told or depicted, be it factual or fictional, realism in both cases depends upon the telling rather than the told. A realistic novel or painting may be full of mistakes while a fantastic painting or novel may be, metaphorically, true or right. *Gulliver's Travels* is unrealistic no matter how true in the way fiction can be true; and a painting by an academic novice will be realistic no matter how wrong. Realism is a matter of the familiarity of symbols used in the telling; truth is a matter of what is told, literally or metaphorically, by means of symbols familiar or fantastic.

"Realism" may of course be used in other ways; but under none of the well-grounded interpretations does realism either imply or follow from rightness.

There are no fictive worlds.

Although some fiction consists of statements, literally false but perhaps metaphorically true, about actual persons, things, and events, most fiction seems to be about fictive persons, things, and events or about imaginary and even impossible beings and entities. Works of fiction, we often hear, are about fictive worlds. But strictly speaking, fiction cannot be about anything nonactual, since there is nothing nonactual, no merely-possible or impossible worlds; for saying that there is something fictive but not actual amounts to saying *that there is something such that there is no such thing.* Thus there are no pictures *of* unicorns or stories *about* ghosts but only unicorn-pictures and ghost-stories.

Fiction, then, no matter how false or how far-out, is about what is actual when about anything at all. There are no fictive worlds. The litterateur pained by that deprivation may or may not be comforted when I add that neither is there any such thing as the actual world. Since there are conflicting truths, there are many worlds if any, but no such thing as *the* world (see II,1 above).

Fiction must be and nonfiction may be literally false; both may be metaphorically true or false. Nonfiction and fiction do not differ in that the one but not the other is about actual things.

Both are about actual things if anything; and different works of either kind may be about the same or different actual worlds.

Not all literal, literary falsehood is fiction.

Although all fiction is literal, literary falsehood, the converse does not hold. Literature includes not only fiction but some biographies and histories, and among these some are partly or wholly false. And while literal falsity, requisite for fiction, is a literary defect in history, falsity does not disqualify a history as a literary work; for as noted earlier, a work of art need not be a good work of art.

But does the false, purported history qualify as nonfiction? If we bear in mind the frequency of human error and remember that a conjunction is false if any component of it is, so that a history with one false statement is itself false, we may well suspect that most literary works, histories as well as novels, are literal falsehoods. The difference among literary works between fiction and nonfiction thus seems to become less a matter of overall literal truth or falsity than of percentage of true and false component sentences. The novel containing a high percentage of literally true statements (Doctorow's *Ragtime* perhaps?) approaches nonfiction; the history with a high percentage of false statements (Carlyle's *French Revolution* perhaps?) approaches fiction. Pure fiction and pure nonfiction are rare.

These five simple theses may seem obvious or shocking. Neglect of them, I think, has often hindered understanding of what fiction is and does.

4. THREE TYPES OF REALISM

A typical English eighteenth-century portrait is more realistic, according to prevalent Western usage, than a Picasso showing three sides of a head at once or an El Greco accentuating upward swirls; and a sketch of the Piazza della Signoria drawn according to standard rules of perspective is more realistic than another drawn according to reversed or otherwise transformed rules. Greater realism here does not imply greater accuracy or infor-

mativeness. The two sketches may convey exactly the same information, and the Picasso and El Greco supply information the
English portrait does not. Moreover, a sketch drawn generally in
standard perspective but with several errors is more realistic than
a sketch in reversed perspective with no errors; and the pictures
that sometimes appear as games with such captions as "Find fifteen mistakes in this picture" are invariably realistic. Realism in
all these cases depends upon familiarity; the pictures in the ac-
customed, standard mode of representation count as the more
realistic.

"Realism", though, has another use as well. Practice palls; and
a new mode of representation may be so fresh and forceful as to
achieve what amounts to a revelation (*LA*, pp. 37–38). This was
true for standard Western perspective when it was invented during the Renaissance, and no less true for modes that broke away
from that system, such as the Oriental mode when rediscovered
by late-nineteenth-century French painters, and various modes
developed by later artists.

Although realism thus may sometimes be associated with revelation, this should not be taken to imply that representation of
any sort consists of faithful reporting on 'the real world'. For
there is, I maintain, no such thing as the real world, no unique,
ready-made, absolute reality apart from and independent of all
versions and visions. Rather, there are many right world-versions, some of them irreconcilable with others; and thus there are
many worlds if any. A version is not so much made right by a
world as a world is made by a right version. Obviously rightness
has therefore to be determined otherwise than by matching a
version with a world. My relativism, which nevertheless recognizes the difference between right and wrong versions, does not
stop with representation and vision and realism and resemblance
but goes through to reality as well.

Concerning the relation between representations and beliefs,
I cannot agree with Menachem Brinker[9] that "a distinction between *representing* and *seeing*, between *artistic conventions* on the one

9. The present section began as a comment on "Verisimilitude, Conventions, and Beliefs" by Menachem Brinker, *New Literary History* 14 (1983)
253–267, but developed into a somewhat broader discussion of realism.

hand and *beliefs* on the other" is "a conceptual necessity".[10] Seeing is as relative to symbol system, to conceptual schemes, as
variable with habit and invention, as is representation. The innocent eye is a myth long dead. And beliefs, far from standing as
independent criteria for judging representations *are themselves
versions,* and they interact in various ways with other versions. A
belief is an accepted version; an accepted sentential version is a
belief; and an accepted representation is to a verbal belief as a
picture is to a description. Beliefs are in symbols of one kind or
another and are no less 'conventional' than other versions.

Realism is not always a matter of familiarity or of revelation.[11]
Hieronymous Bosch's *Garden of Delight,* standard enough in mode
of representation, is hardly realistic but is rather, by virtue of its
subject-matter, fantastic. Realism of the sort missing here would
seem, speaking very loosely, to depend upon depiction of actual
as contrasted with imaginary beings, things, or events, rather
than upon mode of depiction. A Dürer and a Bracque portrait of
an actual person are both realistic in this sense, while even a
Dürer drawing of a dragon is not. Where literary works are concerned, this third sort of realism often takes precedence over the
others. The distinction between a realistic and an unrealistic
story usually lies rather in what is said than in how. The differences that make *Crime and Punishment* more realistic than
Grimm's *Fairy Tales* are rather in the told than in the telling.

But there is a catch here. For two reasons, works that are unrealistic in this third way cannot be identified with those representing nonexistent things, beings, or events.

In the first place, there is nothing that does not exist, no unicorns or centaurs or fairies or dragons to be depicted or described. Strictly speaking, Bosch's painting does not depict
monsters, or the tapestries in the Cloisters depict a unicorn; for
there are no such monsters and there is no unicorn. Rather the
tapestries are unicorn-pictures and the Bosch a monsters-picture.

10. See further: above, I,3; *LA*, I,8; *PP*, III,6; and also Ernst Gombrich *The
Image and the Eye* (Ithaca, N.Y.: Cornell University Press, 1982), pp. 279–287.
11. Consideration of the third kind of realism to be discussed here was
prompted partly by a reading of Charles Rosen and Henri Zerner, "What Is,
and Is Not Realism", *New York Review of Books* 29 (1982) 21–26; and the sequel,
"Enemies of Realism", same, pp. 26–33.

We can as readily sort pictures into unicorn-pictures, monsters-pictures, etc. as we can sort furniture into desks, tables, etc. without their denoting anything and without any available rules or definitions for such sorting. Likewise, Grimm's stories are not strictly tales about fairies (for there are no fairies) but are rather fairy tales.[12]

In the second place, many soandso-pictures and soandso-descriptions that denote no actual soandsos are realistic in the third way; even the most realistic fiction may describe no actual people and relate no actual events. *Rabbit Run* is realistic while *Alice in Wonderland* is not, even though Harry Angstrom is as fictive as the March Hare. Whether a story actually tells of soandsos or is only a soandso-story determines whether it is fiction or history but not whether it is realistic or not. What, then, does make the difference? The answer must again be in terms not of what the pictures and stories denote but in terms of what denotes them, not in terms of how they sort things but in terms of how they are themselves sorted. Just as pictures denoting nothing sort readily into centaur-pictures and unicorn-pictures and monsters-pictures and Northwest Passage maps, so they sort into more comprehensive groups such as mythical-object-pictures, imaginary-landscape-pictures, etc. and into such still larger groups as real-object-pictures and fictive-object-pictures. Real-object-pictures and real-object-descriptions may as in the case of Harry-Angstrom-descriptions be fictive, denoting nothing; and fictive-object-pictures and fictive-object-descriptions may as in the case of a picture of Napoleon as a dragon denote some person or object. A fictional story is realistic in the third way, then, to the extent that it is a real-object-story even though not a story of any real objects. Admittedly, I have no more set forth principles that effect the sorting into real-object-pictures or -descriptions and fictive-object-pictures or -descriptions than I have set forth principles that effect the sorting into centaur-pictures and unicorn-pictures. In both cases the principles, the similarities and differences that matter, are to be accounted for by the sortings rather than accounting for them.

Realism of the third kind, we are inclined to say, depends on

12. For further explanation see *LA*, I,5, and *PP*, V,2.

the nature of the subject-matter; but since pure fiction denotes nothing, mustn't such realism depend upon features of the pictures or story, not upon anything depicted or described? Although, speaking strictly and literally, pure fiction tells of nothing, we can nevertheless distinguish between the telling and the told; that is, sorting of fiction according to what is told differs from sorting according to how it is told. In this somewhat oblique sense, the realism here in question depends upon the subject-matter, upon the told rather than upon the telling.

When I say that pure fiction denotes nothing, I am speaking of its literal application. Taken literally, *Don Quixote* describes no one—there never was or will be the Man of La Mancha—but taken metaphorically, *Don Quixote* describes many of us who battle windmills (or windbags). A fantastic allegory, though an unrealistic fictive-person-story when read literally, may be a realistic real-person-story when taken metaphorically (see III,1 above).

Realism, like reality, is multiple and evanescent, and no one account of it will do.

5. ON BEING IN STYLE

Some questions that I did not consider in my discussion of style (*WW*,II) have been posed by Anita Silvers.[13] I was concerned only with what is meant by saying that a work is in a given style. Such questions as whether a work may have more style than another or be very stylish or without style did not arise. In order not to infuriate Professor Silvers, I shall refrain from suggesting that these are peculiarly feminine questions.

Before I discuss them, two matters need clarification. Readers of the Silvers discussion should be warned that she uses "signature" here differently from the way I ordinarily use it in *Ways of Worldmaking*. She uses it metaphorically as equivalent to "style." I use it literally for the artist's name and, by extension, for all other features that contribute to the placing of a work (as to artist, style, period, etc.) *that are not features of style.*

13. "The Secret of Style", *Journal of Aesthetics and Art Criticism* 39 (1981) 268–271.

Second, she somewhat misinterprets my too brief explication of style when I write that "a property . . . counts as stylistic only when it associates a work with one rather than another artist, period, region, school, etc." (p. 34). I should have written "when it associates a work *with the other works* of one rather than another artist, etc.". A stylistic feature, in my view, is a feature that is exemplified by the work and that contributes to the placing of the work in one among certain significant bodies of work. Characteristic features of such bodies of work—not features of an artist or his personality, or a place or period or its character—constitute style.

Most works are in many styles, varying in specificity and intersecting in various ways: a given painting may be at once in Picasso's style, in his Blue Period style, in the French style, in the twentieth-century style, in Western style, and so on. Silvers suggests that some works, such as television productions, are in no style at all. If so, that is because significant bodies of work have not been picked out and dignified as style-classes. But is there any general measure of degree of stylishness? What is meant by saying that one work has more style than another? The difference can hardly lie in the number of style-classes the works belong to. It lies rather, I think, in the comparative prominence that the stylistic features take on in relation to other features and functions of the works. In a routine picture illustrating an expository text, what counts is what is represented; any stylistic features such a picture may have are inconspicuous, and its exemplification of them matters little. On the other hand, in some inferior mannerist paintings, exemplification of a style may be about all that matters. Underemphasis and overemphasis of style alike are both aesthetic faults. A greater work, such as an El Greco painting, may no less powerfully exemplify a notable style while functioning equally effectively in other aesthetically significant ways.

Incidentally, to be stylish in the context of fashion in clothing is to be in the latest style. This comes under our general formula; for in fashion, being up-to-date is the measure of the transient importance of a style.

*   *   *

Whether a predicate applies to a given thing often depends, Mark Sagoff reminds us, on the realm of discourse.[14] What is small, or green, in one realm may be large, or yellow, in another. And he points out how trouble may arise as much from introduction of deviant 'unnatural' or unentrenched realms as from use of deviant nonprojectible 'grue-like' predicates. We should perhaps also note, though this may be less pertinent to Sagoff's present inquiry, that even when the realm—that is, the logical sum of the extensions of all the predicates of the schema in question—remains constant, the applicability of a predicate is still relative to the composition of the schema in question—that is, to the set of alternatives contemplated. For instance, whether a given disk among a dozen counts as red may depend on whether we are sorting into red and non-red disks, or into red, pink, etc. disks (*LA*, pp. 71–72).

Sagoff goes on to distinguish between, so to speak, general-ordering and other predicates. A general-ordering predicate such as "is taller than" provides a single order embracing all elements in the domains of such more special predicates as "is a taller man than", "is a taller building than", etc. In contrast, sortal predicates may not provide any ordering; and a predicate such as "is more skillful than" provides only orders within each of the several domains of such more special predicates as "is a more skillful carpenter than", "is a more skillful chessplayer than", etc. The requirements for being a tall man are different from those for being a tall building; but while men and buildings can be positively compared for tallness within the broad realm of objects, carpenters and chessplayers cannot be likewise compared for skill. Of course, one might set up some arbitrary correlation among special orders of skill, say by equating the least and most skillful carpenters with the least and most skillful chessplayers; but this is altogether different from the nonarbitrary ordering by which almost any building is taller than almost any man.

The point Sagoff makes here—for example, when he says "someone can be a *skillful* baseball player and a *clumsy* electrician

14. "Historical Authenticity", *Erkenntnis* 12 (1978) 83–93.

without defying the law of contradiction"—has arisen recently in several contexts. My reply to a paper by Robert Nozick (IV,7 below) consisted of remarking that a man may be a good governor and a bad opera singer. And Joseph Ullian and I have recently had to deal (III,7 above) with the fact that a statement about Jones may be true without being true about Jones, and moreover that a statement may be true about Jones without being true. But this is a digression.

Sagoff suggests that aesthetic predicates tend not to be of the general-ordering kind, but to be sortal or at most special-ordering. This, while hardly circumscribing very narrowly the class of aesthetic predicates, seems not implausible in view of, for example, the difficulty of comparing the aesthetic qualities of the Taj Mahal with those of a Sesshu painting.

A second characteristic of aesthetic predicates is that they tend to cut across our entrenched scientific and everyday categories. This poses a problem: on the one hand, we are justly warned of the disastrous results of admitting bizarre, deviant categories and predicates; on the other, we must recognize that the ability to relate things in a novel way, to discern neglected affinities and contrarieties, to transcend the bounds of the commonplace, is fundamental to comprehension and creation in the arts. And to discovery in the sciences as well; for the problem is entirely parallel to that of allowing for novel categories and predicates in science while banning troublemakers like "grue". Consideration of parent predicates, inherited entrenchment, and overhypotheses (FFF, pp. 118–119) are relevant in the case of the aesthetic problem as well; but anything like a full and final answer will take time.

As Sagoff points out, *interpretation* in the arts is largely a matter of calling attention to just those subtle but significant features that, because they transgress habitual sortings, may not be readily evident. He writes:

Notice that an *interpretation,* insofar as it can be said to differ from a *description,* . . . tends to go outside entrenched reference classes in order to focus attention on aesthetically interesting relations between the objects and others with which it is not usually associated.

Sagoff then comes to a matter that, though he does not so present it, threatens to bring out an uncomfortable consequence of taking *Languages of Art* in combination with "The Status of Style" (*WW*, II). I argue in the former that the difference between an original painting and a forgery of it, even though detectable only by elaborate scientific examination, constitutes an aesthetic difference that may in time come to be easily seen. If the difference is thus aesthetic and such as to distinguish the genuine work from, let us say, the much later non-genuine one, then the difference qualifies, by the criteria of "The Status of Style", as stylistic. Therefore, Sagoff concludes, no genuine work and a forgery of it can have the same stylistic properties or be in the same style. A less friendly writer would have flaunted this argument as a devastating objection. For by any reasonable standard, what could be closer in style than an original and an almost indiscernibly different imitation of it?

This would disturb me more than it seems to disturb Sagoff; but the argument is faulty in two respects. In the first place, a style is normally a complex property that can be divided into many stylistic properties. Two works may differ in one or more of these component stylistic properties and yet share others. Thus even though original and copy differ in some stylistic property, they may have others in common. But can the two works be *in the same style?* Styles intersect and range from the quite general to the quite specific. We may speak of Corot's style, or his early style, or his style of a given year, or his landscape style, or his late landscape style, or his Roman landscape style; of French style, or nineteenth-century French style, European style, Western style, post-mediaeval style, and so on. Two pictures may both be in one, or several, of these styles without both, or either, being in others. In a sense, almost any two pictures are in the (i.e., some) same style and in (some) two different styles. What styles are in question in a given case has to be determined by practice, stipulation, or context. Clearly, although the original and an almost indistinguishable copy made far away from it in time and place differ in some stylistic property and are even in some two different styles, they are in a more usual and important sense very much in the same style.

6. ON SYMPTOMS OF THE AESTHETIC

Some pertinent questions about my choice of symptoms of the aesthetic have been raised by Alan Nagel.[15] At the start, I must emphasize that the choice is tentative. In general, a symptom is neither a necessary nor a sufficient condition but rather a feature that we think may, in conjunction with others, make more probable the presence of a given disease or other notable state. And I do not even claim that the symptoms of the aesthetic I list are conjunctively sufficient or disjunctively necessary, though I doubt that what is aesthetic often lacks all of them. Choice of the symptoms perhaps belongs to an early stage in a search for a definition that will derive from and yet must drastically reform an especially chaotic usage. Thus discussion of symptoms of the aesthetic cannot be carried on in terms of proofs of adequacy and conclusive counterexamples. All I can do is to indicate some of the considerations that led to my choice.

The question why referentiality of any and every sort does not count as a symptom is easily answered. The features selected are those thought to be helpful in differentiating aesthetic from other symbolic functioning and symbols; that is, as Nagel conjectures, "referentiality names the field itself" wherein the aesthetic is to be distinguished. But this, as he points out, raises acutely the question: "is exemplification *as a symptom* so clearly any more to the point than denotation or expression?" Since expression involves exemplification, however, albeit of a property metaphorically rather than literally possessed, the question narrows to why *exemplification* but not denotation is taken as a symptom.

The answer is that exemplification is often the most striking feature distinguishing literary from nonliterary texts: poems, novels, short stories, from scientific treatises, cookbooks, and annual reports. In a literary work what usually counts is not only a story told but also how it is told. Much the same is true of the difference among representational pictures between serviceable illustrations and works of art. Rhyme, rhythm, and other pat-

15. " 'Or as a Blanket': Some Comments and Questions on Exemplification", *Journal of Aesthetics and Art Criticism* 39 (1981) 264–266.

terns exemplified, and feelings and other properties expressed, count for much in most works of art, but for little in scientific or practical discourse, whether verbal of pictorial. Of course, exemplification occurs in many a nonaesthetic context—we use examples all the time; and I am not denying that expert revelatory description or depiction or exposition can constitute art. Nevertheless, exemplification qualifies as a symptom in that its presence is often the most marked difference between the aesthetic and the nonaesthetic.

Relative *repleteness* is listed among the symptoms of the aesthetic because it draws the crucial and delicate distinction illustrated in *Languages of Art* by the difference between a stock market chart and a Hokusai drawing of Mount Fujiyama. The lines may match exactly; but in the chart, variations in the thickness and shading of the line do not matter, while in the drawing every variation in every aspect of the line does matter. The premium in a work of art seems to be on repleteness; in a diagram, on attenuation.

The rationale for taking *syntactic* and *semantic density* as symptoms is somewhat different. They may seem unpromising as signs of the aesthetic since, for example, no text whether literary or not is syntactically dense, while all are semantically dense. Thus choice of these symptoms cannot be based on any supposition that the aesthetic is more often than not syntactically dense or that the nonaesthetic more often than not lacks semantic density. Rather the thought is that the syntactically and semantically dense symbols and systems we encounter and use are more often than not aesthetic; that within the aesthetic more often than elsewhere we find the dense. Thus density, especially when combined with other symptoms, suggests the aesthetic.

Multiple and complex reference, the fifth symptom, was added after *Languages of Art* was written.[16] Scientific and practical discourse, verbal or pictorial, normally aims at singularity and directness, avoiding ambiguity and complicated routes of reference. But in the arts, multiple and complex reference of all sorts—from simple ambiguity of denotation to reference through

16. WW, pp. 67–68.

one or more straight or tortuous chains traversing several levels—is common and is often a powerful instrument. Though not a universal or exclusive feature, it is a symptom of the aesthetic.

Other features, such as figurativeness and fictiveness, have sometimes been proposed as additional symptoms. But metaphor in some stage of decay so permeates almost all language that figurativeness strikes me as having little symptomatic value. As for fictiveness, not only are many nonfictive texts works of art; but abstract works, not denoting at all, are not fictive. This of itself would not necessarily rule out fictiveness as a symptom. What does seem to me to disqualify it is that a fictive work always refers by exemplification or expression or through a referential chain. Fictiveness would thus add nothing to a list of symptoms that already includes exemplification and complex reference.

Looking over all these symptoms, I notice certain interesting affinities among them. Three are properties required to be absent from what I have defined as a notation, and the other two would be extraneous and usually troublesome in a notation. All five are features that tend to reduce transparency, that tend to require concentration upon the symbol to determine what it is and what it refers to. Where exemplification occurs, we have to inhibit our habit of passing at once from symbol to what is denoted. Repleteness requires attention to comparatively many feature of the symbol. Dense systems, where every difference in a feature makes a difference, call for an endless search to find what symbol we have and what it symbolizes.

Have we here then a neat, complete, inevitable, and inviolable set of symptoms? Not at all. None is always present in the aesthetic or always absent from the nonaesthetic; and even presence or absence of all gives no guarantee either way. Nor do the symptoms offer a way of measuring to what *degree* a symbol or function is aesthetic; to have more of the symptoms is not to be more aesthetic. All we have here are the hesitant results of groping toward a more adequate characterization of the aesthetic; and the symptoms stand in somewhat the same relation to such a characterization as lines drawn in the mud to a surveyor's plan. Furthermore, these symptoms are symptoms of aesthetic function, not of aesthetic merit; symptoms of art, not of good as against bad art. Being a work of art no more implies being a good work than being a sentence implies being a true one. (See further IV,7 below.)

7. VIRTUE CONFINED

Some years ago, Robert Nozick[17] attacked my account (LA, pp. 255–261) of the relationship between being aesthetic and having aesthetic merit. I had written that aesthetic merit requires being aesthetic and being cognitively effective. He argued that had Newton's theories been presented in a bad poem rather than in a prose treatise, that poem—being aesthetic and being cognitively effective—would be aesthetically meritorious according to my criterion.

What he seems to have overlooked is that something may be good in one way and bad in another. Obviously a man may govern well or sing folk songs well and sing opera badly; the excellence of his governing or folksinging is entirely compatible with the badness of his opera singing. Likewise, obviously, a text may function well as a treatise and badly as a poem. Strictly, a way a thing functions symbolically, rather than the thing itself, qualifies or fails to qualify as aesthetic; and aesthetic excellence consists in cognitive effectiveness of a work when functioning aesthetically. When so functioning, a work may be good or bad; very good, mediocre, and very bad works may be equally aesthetic. Sadly, most works of art are bad.

In short, aesthetic excellence depends not only upon how and how well but also upon what a work symbolizes—upon its contribution to effective organization of a world. How that contribution is to be judged, what makes for aesthetic rightness (or scientific or other rightness), is no easy question (see WW,VII). But the first step toward dealing with it must be to avoid mistak-

17. In "Goodman, Nelson, on Merit, Aesthetic", Journal of Philosophy 69 (1972) 783–785.

ing a classification for a commendation. Being aesthetic does not imply being aesthetically good. If virtue is to remain unsullied, it must be carefully cloistered.

8. ON THE IDENTITY OF WORKS OF ART

Two matters dealt with in *Languages of Art* need to be clarified or stressed: the distinction between autographic and allographic arts, and the notion of identification of works or their instances.

Concerning the distinction between autographic and allographic arts or works (*LA*, III, 3-4), the first point is that this distinction does not coincide with that between singular and multiple arts; for some multiple arts, such as etching, are autographic. Second, while the distinction between autographic and allographic arts is generally allied with the distinction between arts where there may and those where there may not be forgeries of particular works, the autographic-allographic distinction is not so *defined* and could obtain in a world of inventive angels free of imitative instincts or ill intent. Third, while availability of a notation is usually what establishes an art as allographic, mere availability of a notation is neither a necessary nor a sufficient condition. What *is necessary* is that identification of the or an instance of a work[18] be independent of the history of production; a notation as much codifies as creates such an independent criterion. That a notation is *not sufficient* to make an art allographic is illustrated in the use of a library-like system for numbering paintings.[19] Fourth, not every art can be classed as autographic or as allographic. This classification applies only where we have some means of sorting objects or events into works—that is, where there is some criterion for identity of a work. Sometimes, as in some of Cage's music that uses nonnotational sketches in place of scores, we have no such definitive criterion and so in effect no works and no distinction between autographic and allo-

18. In a singular art such as painting, the work may be thought of as its own sole instance.
19. Under a system used by many museums the 21st acquisition of 1976 is labeled "76.21".

graphic, or even between singular and multiple, works. Finally, I do not at all maintain that whether a given art is autographic or allographic arises from anything more than a tradition that might have been different and may change. Factors such as the ephemeral character of performances and the participation of many persons may favor an art's becoming allographic; but that is far from saying that any art must always have been or forever will be allographic, or autographic.

As for identification of a work, we are here concerned with determination that a given object or event is an instance of a given work. What such determination involves may vary considerably with how the work is specified; for example, determination that a given event is a performance of Haydn's Symphony No. 101 requires determination both of compliance with a score and of authorship and title of that score. But for distinguishing allographic from autographic works, all that counts is whether or not identity of the work—quite apart from any particular question of author or opus—is independent of history of production.

Perhaps I did not make this clear enough in *Languages of Art*. At any rate, Richard Wollheim misunderstands the point, I think, when he argues that identification of allographic as well as of autographic works involves history of production.[20] Of course for any work, autographic or allographic, determination of authorship, opus, period, and so on, are aspects of history of production. What distinguishes an allographic work is that identification of an object or event as an instance of the work depends not at all upon how or when or by whom that object or event was produced. An inscription of a poem, for example, however produced, need only be correctly spelled; and two inscriptions of the same poem need only be spelled alike. In contrast, an instance of a given etching must have been printed from a given plate; and two instances of the same etching, however alike or different they may look, must be impressions from the same plate.

Wollheim is tempted at one point to go so far as to claim that two identically spelled inscriptions ought to be considered in-

20. "Are the Criteria of Identity that Hold for a Work of Art in Different Arts Aesthetically Relevant?" *Ratio* 20 (1978) 29–48.

stances of different works, but wisely stops short of this. To deny that I have read *Don Quixote* if my copy, though correctly spelled in all details, happens to have been accidentally produced by a mad printer in 1500, or by a mad computer in 1976, seems to me utterly untenable. But further questions do arise here. What constitutes correct spelling needs careful specification; for only in relation to a language is a physical mark a letter, and the same marks may spell different words in different languages. And Borges questions whether even sameness of spelling in the same language is enough to identify a work: did Cervantes and Menard, writing the same words in Spanish, write the same work or even the same text?[21] I am currently (1983) exploring some of these matters for a paper on interpretation and identity.

Wollheim goes on to argue that the criteria of identity for works in different arts have aesthetic importance in that they enter into the artist's theory and thus into his work. I think there is an element of truth in what Wollheim says here but I should want to make some drastic amendments. I am as suspicious of talk about an artist's theory as I am of talk about a speaker's grammatical theory. Some artists and some speakers of a language do have such overt theories; and in a few cases an artist's or speaker's theory may have some recognizable and noninhibiting effect on what he produces. But I think few artists and few speakers have such theories explicitly, and what it could mean to say they have the theories implicitly puzzles me as much as what it would mean to say the planets have the laws of motion implicitly. In all these cases, I suspect, the theory is supplied by a theorist other than the artist, the speaker, or the planets. And I find especially untoward the idea that theory normally plays in the nonverbal arts any such role as Wollheim maintains; for a theory, as I understand it, consists of statements of words. Does Wollheim mean thus to subjugate painting or dance, for example, to language? If not, what does he consider to constitute a theory, or the analog of a theory, in the symbol systems of painting or dance? Works of art do indeed offer nonverbal world-versions

21. Jorge Luis Borges, "Pierre Menard, Author of the Quixote" in *Labyrinths*, trans. James E. Irby (New York: New Directions, 1962), pp. 36–44.

or fragments thereof, but how this leads to the conclusion that criteria for a work's identity enter into the artist's theory and work seems to me to require, at least, some elaborate exposition.

Wollheim also raises the question whether a work of art is identical with or is different from and merely resides, perhaps fleetingly, in its physical manifestations—as a soul is sometimes supposed to inhabit a body. Wollheim defends the latter view. I reject both alternatives in favor of a functional view. Quite clearly a piece of bronze may be a work of art and a bludgeon; a canvas may be a Rembrandt masterpiece and a blanket. But can a physical object and a work be the same? We might equally well ask, but seldom do, whether the bronze and the bludgeon are the same, or the canvas and blanket. The answer indicated seems to be that in both cases we have the same physical objects performing different functions. We need not look for an aesthetic object distinct from the physical vehicle but only distinguish aesthetic from other more practical functions. While no bludgeon is a Rodin and no blanket is a Rembrandt, the same physical object may batter or warm in some contexts and perform the symbolic functions of a work of art in others. As I have suggested elsewhere, we may need to turn our attention from the question "What is art?" to the question "When is art?" (WW, IV). Perhaps this bears also on the Borges problem, resolving it into questions about when a given text in Spanish is the Cervantes and when it is the Menard *Don Quixote*.

9. IMPLEMENTATION OF THE ARTS

Implementation of a work of art may be distinguished from execution—whether in one or two stages—of that work. The novel is completed when written, the painting when painted, the play when performed. But the novel left in a drawer, the painting stacked in a storeroom, the play performed in an empty theater does not fulfill its function. In order to work, the novel must be published in one way or another, the painting shown publicly or privately, the play presented to an audience. Publication, exhibition, production before an audience are means of implementation—and ways that the arts enter into culture. Execution consists of making a work, implementation of making it work (see V,5 below).

So stated, the distinction may seem too obvious to call for much further comment, but the relationship between execution and implementation is in some respects rather complex, and exploration of that relationship touches on some more general questions concerning art.

Under "execution", I include all that goes into the creation of a work, from the first flicker of an idea to the final touch. Although the question how a line between conception and realization can be drawn, especially in one-stage arts, may be of considerable interest, it does not concern me here; "execution" covers the whole process of making a work. Under "implementation", on the other hand, I include all that goes into making a work work; and a work works, in my view, to the extent that it is understood, to the extent that what and how it symbolizes (whether by description or depiction or exemplification or expression or via some longer route—see III,1 above) is discerned and affects the way we organize and perceive a world. Sometimes, I use "implementation" loosely enough to cover attempts at implementation regardless of their success, procedures undertaken to make a work work whether or not they actually do so. For example, framing is a process of implementation even though it sometimes paralyzes rather than activates a painting; and museum exhibition is a means of implementation even when it leaves the works inert.

Now compare the one-stage art of the novel with the two-stage art of etching (IV,8 above, and LA, pp. 112–115). The novel is completed in the manuscript, and all such further steps as printing, promotion, and distribution are processes of implementation. The etching, on the other hand, is not complete when the plate is made, but only when impressions are taken from it; for these prints constitute the only instances of the work. Accordingly, while the printing of a novel is not part of its execution but of its implementation, the printing of an etching is part of its execution, and implementation consists of mounting, framing, exhibiting, promoting, distributing, etc. Insofar as publication is exclusively implementation, publication of a novel includes printing, while publication of an etching does not. In other two-stage arts as well—whether autographic like etching or allographic like scored music—implementation depends upon execution of both stages: a dramatic or musical work exists only if performed, a bronze sculpture only if cast, an architectural work only if built.

In the performing arts, the processes of execution and implementation are temporally intertwined; for the primary working of a play occurs while it is being performed before an audience. That is, presentation of a play to an audience (a matter of implementation) not only requires but occurs during performance (a matter of execution). Although execution normally begins before implementation, implementation (by production planning, promotion, ticket sales) may begin before execution is complete and (by comment and criticism) continue afterward.

Sometimes, though, execution and implementation are even more intimately connected. Consider, for example, the multimedia theater piece Hockey Seen (see III,1 above). Execution of the drawings, of the dance, and of the music are all elements in the execution of the whole, even though the drawings were not made for that purpose. But also execution of the theater piece is a step toward implementation of the drawings. Projection of the drawings in combination with the dance and music is one way of making them work—a way that unlike some others incorporates execution of another work. Nothing here, however, blurs the basic distinction between execution and implementation.

So far we seem to have found that while the line between execution and implementation must be carefully drawn, with due regard to certain differences among the arts, and while implementation of one work may involve execution of another, still execution and implementation are clearly distinct and the former never implies the latter. Offhand, one might suppose further that although execution may occur without implementation, implementation can never occur without execution; for how can what is not yet made be implemented? Surprisingly, this needs closer examination.

A work must, indeed, be executed if it is to be implemented, but that is because we have a *work* at all only through execution—a work is something *made*. Where an object is not an artefact but rather, say, a stone found on a beach (*LA*, pp. 37, 66), implementation may nevertheless occur: for example, as when the stone is mounted and displayed in an art museum. But I do not—as is sometimes supposed—subscribe to any "institutional" theory of art. *Institutionalization is only one, sometimes overemphasized and often ineffectual, means of implementation.* What counts is the functioning rather than any particular way of effecting it. The beach stone may be made to function as art merely through singling it out where it lies and perceiving it as a symbol exemplifying certain forms and other properties. Implementation, clearly, is not restricted to making a work of art work as such, but includes making anything work as art.

Here we begin to perceive that the contrast between execution and implementation is not as stark as we might suppose. For we now see that implementation even without execution may itself be productive—or even, though I dislike the word, creative. It can make a nonwork work as art; it achieves aesthetic functioning. In *Ways of Worldmaking* I suggested that the question "When is art?" may be more fundamental than the question "What is art?" The beach stone is no work of art but under some conditions functions as art; a Rembrandt painting used as a blanket is a work of art but does not then so function. And what constitutes a work of art may have to be defined in terms of its primary or usual or standard function. Function may underlie status.

More than a little experience with works of art is nonaesthetic, and more than a little aesthetic experience is with nonworks. Works of art often do not function as such, and nonworks often do. Although execution and implementation, where both occur, may be distinguished, they make up a continuous process with aesthetic functioning as its end. On the one hand, execution of a *work* is required for its implementation; on the other hand, implementation is the process of bringing about the aesthetic functioning that provides the basis for the notion of a work of art.

V. Art in Action

S ome of my experience relating to implementation of the arts is reflected in this chapter, which begins with a brief account of the aims of Project Zero's basic research into education for the arts. "Explorations in Art Education" is a collaborative report on some aspects of the work of the project during the four years I directed it. "A Message from Mars" is a bitter parody of the mistreatment of the arts in some of our foremost universities. "Art and Ideas" celebrates the career and writing of an original and notable museum director. "The End of the Museum?" was delivered before a huge audience of museum professionals. Most of them resented it thoroughly.

Thus this book, which begins with a paper for a meeting on science policy, ends with a lecture for a meeting on arts policy.

1. NOTES FROM THE UNDERGROUND

"Cognitive" has been a battle cry in psychology and in philosophy of the arts for some decades. The movement it stands for, one of the most liberating and productive in this century, is often decried by behavioristically oriented theorists as nonempirical and unscientific, and widely thought by writers on art to be bent on analyzing the arts to death.

The trouble arises, I think, from a complex of confusions: confusion about cognition, about education, and about art and science. The cognitive approach to education for the arts must

146

surely be condemned if cognition is contrasted with perception, emotion, and all nonlogical and nonlinguistic faculties; or if education is identified exclusively with lecturing, explaining, and providing texts and verbal and numerical exercises; or if art is looked upon as transient amusement for a passive audience, while science is taken as consisting of demonstrations founded upon observation and aimed at practical progress. From its beginning some fifteen years ago Project Zero, a program of basic research into education for the arts, has had to combat these confusions.[1]

For the cognitivist, cognition includes learning, knowing, gaining insight and understanding, by all available means. Developing sensory discrimination is as cognitive as inventing complex numerical concepts or proving theorems. Mastering a motor skill involves making subtle kinaesthetic distinctions and connections. Coming to understand a painting or a symphony in an unfamiliar style, to recognize the work of an artist or school, to see or hear in new ways, is as cognitive an achievement as learning to read or write or add. Even the emotions function cognitively: in organizing a world, felt contrasts and kinships, both subtle and salient, are no less important than those seen or heard or inferred.

Accordingly, for the cognitivist education includes all ways and means of preserving, motivating, fostering, developing such abilities as are involved in cognition in the broadest sense: that is, in the advancement of the understanding. The need for transcending stunted prevalent notions of education is underlined by Sherman Lee when he writes:

The art museum is not primarily an "educational" institution in the current limited interpretation of the word . . . rather it performs a kind of educational function presently unrecognized by legislators and even educators. In showing or juxtaposing visual images, the art museum

1. I founded Project Zero in 1967 at the Harvard Graduate School of Education and directed it for four years. Since then it has been directed by David Perkins and Howard Gardner. The research is conducted by a varying group of psychologists, philosophers, and others, paid and unpaid, and has been reported in a number of books and papers. See further V,2 below.

provides an education unfamiliar to a word- and sound-oriented society. For the most part visually illiterate, our society defines education
in logical sentences—acceptable words and sounds . . . however, the
museum . . . by existing—preserving and exhibiting works of art— . . .
is educational in the broadest and best sense, though it never utters a
sound or prints a word.[2]

Not only showing and juxtaposing visual images, though, but the
varied means of improving performance of all kinds, whether in
tuning pianos or engines or in dramatic acting or in athletics or in
the practice of law or management, are means of education; and
some may prove effective beyond their customary applications.

Finally, the cognitivist rejects all the popular clichés that put
the arts (as evaluative, subjective, emotive, passive contemplation yielding only pleasure) in opposition to the sciences (as factual, objective, rational, active inquiry yielding new knowledge).
Rating works of art or scientific discoveries according to their
greatness matters much less than comprehending and projecting
them. Delight is a dividend that comes with the achievement of
new insight by means of either science or art. Effective new ways
of seeing or hearing or feeling as well as effective new scientific
conceptions and theories are aspects of growth in the making
and grasping of our worlds. The genuine and significant differences between art and science are compatible with their common
cognitive function; and the philosophy of science and the philosophy of art are embraced within epistemology conceived as the
philosophy of the understanding.

These major reconceptions call for massive reform of research
into education for the arts. Recognition of kinship between the
arts and the sciences requires investigation into their common
features and their specific differences. Education for the arts, like
education for the sciences, is seen as focused not upon 'creativity' or the production of geniuses but upon developing the skills
involved in understanding and discovery, and upon providing
motivation and conditions for the exercise of these skills.

A study of how to develop the appropriate skills must begin
with a study of how skills are to be identified and classified. Only

2. In "Art Museums and Education", *Art International* 21 (1977) 48–51. See
also note 7 below.

in terms of some such initial conceptual apparatus can we ask pertinent questions about ways of fostering particular skills or about how improvement in a given skill may enhance or inhibit another. Since both science and art consist very largely in the processing of symbols, an analysis and classification of types of symbol systems—linguistic, notational, diagrammatic, pictorial, etc.—and of literal and figurative symbolic functions—denotation, exemplification, expression, and reference through chains of these—provides an indispensable theoretical background. It enables us to deal, for example, with such central and neglected matters as the definition of language and the significant differences between a description and a depiction and between a literary and a scientific work.

All such philosophical analysis is an anathema to most aestheticians but perhaps less abhorrent than the next step: bringing brain physiology to bear on research into arts education. Theoretical relationships derived from the conceptual framework need to be examined in the light of conjoint or separate impairment of these skills under various brain injuries. That among such apparently alike skills as reading words and reading numerals and reading musical scores some may be lost while others are preserved moves us to seek the relevant differences among these tasks. That two apparently disparate skills vanish together may point to a kinship that requires formulation. Conceptual apparatus and clinical experience must be tested against each other, and often refined or reinterpreted (see I,4 above). Differential impairment of seemingly like skills may, for instance, call for an analysis of 'reading' into many component skills; and some of these may also be components of the skill of understanding pictures or musical works. Furthermore, some skills involved in the arts may also be involved in quite other activities; and some means of education familiar only in other fields may prove appropriate for the arts.

Research into arts education thus tends to expand into a general study of how human beings learn, know, understand, but with this distinctive feature: that human abilities and activities in the arts are seen to be an integral part of that study.

Whether cognitively oriented or not, research into art education is widely disparaged on the ground that the practicing educator in the particular arts—the master draftsman, the coach of singers, the teacher of acting or dancing or architecture—knows very well how to get results and is unlikely to profit much from studies by those who are not artists. But however well grounded the claim may be, the condemnation is mistaken. For one major responsibility of art education is to induce attitudes conducive to persistent work in any art. And as the student undertaking serious study of a science needs to be able to read intelligently, calculate, and have some experience with experimentation and inference and with the excitement of inquiry and discovery, so the student undertaking serious work in an art needs to be able to see or hear intelligently and have some experiences with inquisitive perception and creative imagination and with the excitement of new insight and invention in the arts. On these matters, the basic research I have been describing can, even from its early stages, give the educator some guidance.

Moreover, because in our culture the arts are not really taken seriously, and their whole nature and function is widely misunderstood and often misrepresented, even by their most vocal advocates, the integration of the arts into our concept of the cognitive and thus into the overall educational process is vitally important for students who are not to become artists at all. Here even the initial formulation of the cognitively oriented program of research makes an urgently needed contribution. How works of art, and through them our worlds, may be comprehended and created must be part of basic education for the millions of us who will never be artists of any kind. Why? Because this will equip us better for survival and success? Rather, because advancement of the understanding is what makes survival and success worthwhile.

2. EXPLORATIONS IN ART EDUCATION

Background and Beginnings

The ultimate purpose of Project Zero is advancement of the arts through improved education of artists, audiences, and management. As compared with education in other fields, education for the arts is sparse, sporadic, and chaotic. Programs and passionate convictions abound, but communicable general principles for planning sound programs and evaluating them are sadly wanting. We have been seeking such principles by examining the processes and human abilities peculiarly involved in the production or comprehension of one or more of the arts. Research so basic is inevitably long-range, with little probability of early applicable results. Yet in the course of our study to date some promising hypotheses have gained support.

To say even this much is to arouse antagonism. "If such research were carried out, the arts would be destroyed" is a characteristic comment. Many are convinced that everything related to the arts is by its very nature idiosyncratic; and that any analysis, any investigation of education—even education itself—is antithetical to the arts. Some of the opposition and obstacles to our effort will be discussed below; but we must warn here against hasty conclusions as to our approach and its feasibility. We are not looking for mathematical formulas for nurturing abilities in the arts; rather we are studying the various possible ways that education may be made more helpful—or at least less damaging—to such abilities. We ask that our work be judged not by antecedent prejudices but by its progress and results, tentative and partial as these may still be.

We began near zero (hence our name) with little more than a conviction of the importance of the task and some tentative notions as to where to direct our attention first. Bits of evidence, conjectures, apparently remote studies, perplexing questions, have come gradually to relate to and illuminate each other. These have suggested new hypotheses and lines of thought that have in turn brought to bear the results of other, often apparently remote, studies. If we have not done nearly what needs to be done, we at least know much better what we are doing. Progress has been made in draining the swamp, driving some pylons, starting foundations, erecting scaffolding, and here and there putting in a door or a window.

A task as comprehensive and uncharted as ours required a theoretical framework that might later be elaborated, revised, or discarded. This need was filled by an approach to a theory of symbols detailed in *Languages of Art,* completed during the first year of the Project. Much of knowing, acting, and understanding in the arts, the sciences, and life in general involves the use—the interpretation, application, invention, revision—of symbol systems. Such symbol systems may be classified into kinds according to certain significant characteristics. By identifying the kinds of symbol systems involved in a given phase of a particular artistic activity, we have gained some clues as to the skills required as well as to ways of discerning and developing those skills. For example, the peculiar differences between linguistic and nonlinguistic symbols—once they are disentangled from the pseudo-difference between verbal and visual symbols—may point to differences in the kind of training required to handle them.

This general approach has suggested many of our studies and has led to the discovery of some intriguing relationships between our theoretical analysis and the work of psychologists and neurologists. These leads may well throw light on fundamental aspects of education for the arts. But our research has by no means been constrained by or confined to this way of thinking. Indeed, the Project has pursued several other lines of investigation that seemed essential for a comprehensive approach to education in the arts. For example, we have organized a taxonomy of educational methods. We have visited several institutions with active programs in the arts in order to observe their methods and examine their philosophies. We have given considerable attention to problem-solving, which has impressed us as a process much more central to artistic endeavor than is generally thought. We have examined the perception of rhythm in music, and the role of rhythm as an organizing force in human development. The basic psychology of human vision and its implications for the visual arts have also been topics of analysis and experimentation.

Our inquiry has had to proceed, roughly, from our own experience and theoretical study to the formulation and clarification of relevant problems, then to the analysis of these into more manageable specific questions, and then to pertinent and directed observation and experimentation. In some aspects of our program we have already reached the experimental stage; in others, further work is still needed in crystalizing the conceptual apparatus in terms of which the crucial questions are to be framed.

Opposition and Obstacles

Although we began by asking what had already been done, we soon found ourselves asking rather why so little had been accomplished or even attempted. What explains the dismal past record of failures, frustrations, and omissions?

Much of the trouble has lain in a motley collection of popular prejudices and philosophical fallacies concerning the arts, education, and even research methodology. Perhaps the most pervasive misconceptions construe art as a matter of immediate experience, emotions, and values in contrast with science as a matter of inference, cognition, and fact. The conclusion is drawn either that the arts are unteachable or that methods for teaching immediate awareness, feeling, and appreciation must be sought. This line of thinking seems to us wrong in its conception of arts, in its tacit identification of education with teaching, and in each of its alternative conclusions. In part, it derives from venerable but untenable epistemological dichotomies: the 'given' or immediate versus the inferred or mediate, the emotive versus the cognitive. In part, it derives from isolating the functions of understanding and evaluation from one another, and absurdly assuming that while understanding is ultimate for science, 'appreciation' is ultimate for art. Without arguing the case here, we invite consideration of consequences, for our present inquiry of recognizing that the distinction between mediate and immediate experience may be illusory, that the emotions rather than being antithetical to cognition may be instruments of it, and that appreciation may be as subsidiary to understanding in the arts as in the sciences. Among other things, the problems of education for the arts may come to seem less idiosyncratic, or at least less hopeless; and agreement with the teacher's taste may be dropped as a test of the student's promise and as a measure of his progress.

Serious study of education for the arts has also been stunted and sidetracked by the prevalent notion that the arts are merely instruments of entertainment. Some newspapers list plays, concerts, and exhibitions under "amusements"; and among a week's amusements may be a Bach Mass, *King Lear*, and an exhibition of Goya's *Disasters of War*. No real progress in attitudes toward education can be hoped for when Cézanne's pictures are classed with cookouts, and arts programs with playgrounds. On the other hand, we encounter almost as often the equally detrimental mistake of exalting the arts to a plane far above most human activities, accessible only to an elite.

Reaction against both these extremes has inspired elaborate arguments emphasizing extraneous psychological and practical virtues of training in the arts. It is held to soothe the spirit, sharpen the mind, increase effectiveness in daily pursuits, resolve social tensions, and so on. Whatever merit these arguments may have, they succeed mainly—by their very existence—in fostering the suspicion that the arts are worthless in themselves.

Further confusion results from the frequent mistaking of the problem of education in the arts for the problem of creativity. The study of creativity, whatever it may be, is part but not all or even the major part of our program. Ways of discovering and fostering originality, superior talent, genius, are surely wanted for the arts; but no more so than for the technologies and sciences. That we have no sure method of producing Edisons or Einsteins does not lessen the importance of providing training that they, and scientists and technicians in general, need: training in reading, calculating, solving problems, framing and testing hypotheses, proving theorems. The parallel problems for art still need urgently to be defined and investigated, whatever we are or are not able to do about creativity.

Overemphasis on creativity, emotion, and immediacy has nourished the idea that art is a matter of pure inspiration, that a work blooms suddenly in the artist's consciousness and needs only to be embodied.[3] Rather, we maintain that inspiration—

3. For some examples of this view, see Brewster Ghiselin, ed., *The Creative Process* (New York: Mentor, 1952).

welcome and exciting when it occurs—is usually sporadic and partial; and realization, whether in physics or painting, in medicine or music, is normally an arduous process, straining skill and pertinacity. The romantic identification of art with inspiration discourages serious examination of what is involved in production or understanding of the arts.

Damaging in a different way is the delusion that we have clear and reliable standards for judging the merit of works of art. A sensible measure of success in education for the arts might seem to be the excellence of works subsequently produced or preferred by the students. The trouble is that the criteria of excellence are highly provincial and transient. One cannot confidently endorse a school that produces a generation of Rosa Bonheurs, no matter how evident testimony to success this may seem at a given time and place. Nor is departure from current standards any better measure than conformity; production of work in accordance with or in defiance of whatever canons happen to be locally and temporarily in effect is a dangerous test.

We are not suggesting that there are no standards of artistic merit or that one can forego all judgment of quality of works produced in appraising an educational program. But the standards are too elusive and most judgments too personal to provide the basis for any dependable method of validation. This proves a major problem at the very beginning of our study. In most fields there are reasonably accessible measures of success: winning races or tournaments, making profits, raising standards of living, reducing crime and poverty, reaching the moon. If there is no ready criterion for the goodness of a work of art, how are methods of art education to be evaluated? Part of the answer is that we must depend rather heavily upon antecedent analytical study of how human beings function in performing tasks involved in comprehending and producing works of art. But whatever care we exercise in formulating credible hypotheses, they must be subjected to some experimental control; and finding how to do that will give us some trouble. One reason the urgent and exasperating problem of evaluation has been neglected is that as matters stand almost any effort at education in the arts can plausibly claim success. For, by the well-known Hawthorne effect[4] even pointless or ill-conceived attention may prove an effective placebo in improving performance. Nonetheless, we have reached certain tentative conclusions about evaluation which are detailed below.

A hampering misconception about education rather than, or in addition to, a misconception about art is disclosed in arguments to the effect that because art (for one reason or another) is unteachable, education for the arts is useless or even detrimental. Whatever the truth of the premiss, the conclusion does not follow. Education must not be equated with teaching, or even with schools. Coaching, apprenticeship, demonstration, cooperative assistance, etc. are effective means for the improvement of some abilities. What is unteachable may well be trainable, or amenable to other educational methods. The distinctions and interrelations between the several aspects or modes of education—that is, of inculcating and developing abilities of various kinds—need careful examination. This painstaking analysis and clarification of educational procedure in general is particularly important for progress in our special study.

Some more specialized miscues have resulted from serious but misdirected efforts to deal with particular problems. One example is the current insistence by many arts educators upon contrasting the verbal and the visual. The difference between poems and paintings—between the verbal and the nonverbal—is highly significant. But to characterize this difference by the terms "verbal" and "visual" is to overlook the fact that the verbal is as often visual (e.g., in reading) as not, and that the nonvisual (e.g., auditory) is often nonverbal. An unhappy synecdoche has made for a mix-up.

Convictions and Conjectures

Pointing to all these misconceptions implies some underlying positive principles. Some attitudes, hunches, and hypotheses

4. See further V,5 below. The Hawthorne effect was first described in Elton Mayo, *Human Problems of Industrial Civilization* (Cambridge, Mass.: Harvard University Press, 1933), pp. 53–73.

pervading our study have operated from the beginning; others have emerged in the course of our work. Some were convictions; some conjectures; but all were subject to revision as the study proceeded.

Underlying our approach are two acknowledged prejudices; that art needs no justification in terms of anything else; and that what counts is quality rather than quantity—better pictures rather than more, better insight than bigger audiences.

Like understanding and discovery of all sorts—from the simplest perception to the most subtle pattern detection and the most complex conceptual clarification—comprehension and creation in the arts are not matters of passive contemplation or pure inspiration but involve active, constructive processes of discrimination, interrelation, and organization.[5] Accordingly, sensation is no longer isolated from thought, the several senses from one another, or the arts from the sciences. Perception and problem-solving and painting have much in common. Nicolai Bernschtein's work[6] suggests that even the performance of seemingly simple physical tasks may involve mastering complex problems of coordination. We are thus encouraged to examine the skills or abilities involved in all these active processes, look for those most central in the several arts, and ask what educational means are appropriate to develop these abilities. We hope to measure improvement in these abilities in terms of increased success in performing certain specifiable types of tasks.

Education is preparation for the performance of subsequent tasks. It depends essentially upon transfer of learning; what is learned must be applied to further tasks of the same kinds or to tasks of other kinds. This is not to accede to a discredited 'faculty psychology'—to suppose that there is a fixed and fundamental set of atomic skills. Rather, our effort has been to devise a taxonomy of tasks and of abilities to perform them that is serviceable for our particular purposes, and then investigate how develop-

5. See, e.g., Ulric Neisser, *Cognitive Psychology* (New York: Appleton Century Crofts, 1967), pp. 46–104.
6. Nikolai A. Bernschtein, *The Coordination and Regulation of Movements* (Oxford and New York: Pergamon Press, 1967).

ment of some of these abilities may enhance or inhibit the development of others. As suggested above, one clue to such a taxonomy is the recognition that almost all the processes under consideration involve extensive operation with and upon symbols of various kinds. Sentences, gestures, diagrams, and maps are incessantly devised or discovered, applied, interpreted, revised, rejected, supplemented, translated. We have sought to apply the systematization of symbol theory begun in *Languages of Art* to the study of the differences and interrelationships among the abilities involved in the arts.

Art in the Making

The Project, along with its research, has planned and conducted or participated in active educational programs; for example, a series of performance-demonstrations or lecture-performances, and an institute of arts management.

The lecture-performance or performance-demonstration is a means of audience education. Project Zero produced many of these, under the management of Frank Dent, for the Harvard Graduate School of Education, the Harvard community, and the general public. Professional artists conducted the presentations in consultation with the Project research staff. The programs were designed to provide insight into the means by which an artist makes a work of art.

Characteristic of the aims and methods of the series were the six presentations planned for the 1969–70 academic year, under the general title "Art in the Making". In the first, on still photography, Dr. Alfred Guzzetti displayed, side by side, several shots of a subject, and discussed with the audience the comparisons and judgments leading to choice among them for inclusion in a book. Another program, entitled "The Director Who Chooses", offered four different versions of a scene from Arthur Miller's *Death of a Salesman*, two live and two on film. George Hamlin, associate director of the Loeb Drama Center at Harvard, compared the four, revealing places where the several directors' differing conceptions of the play emerged. The last fall presentation featured noted poet and critic I. A. Richards reading from his own works, some of them unfinished, and commenting on problems and opportunities for expression in each.

Modern dance, mime, and music were the themes of the spring presentations. Ann Tolbert choreographed a work in celebration of the centennial of Sanders Theater, a vast nineteenth-century gothic memorial to Harvard's Civil War dead. The particular aim was to illustrate how the setting could be strongly integrated into the work: banisters, moldings, statues, and even the basement of the building itself were utilized in the dance-movements and in other aspects of the presentation. In the second spring offering Jacques Lecoq, director of the School of Mime and Theater Movement in Paris, made his first U.S. appearance in a 'conference-spectacle' on the subject "Mime, Mask, and Contra-Mask". Following analysis of the language of gestures as observed in daily life and translated into the techniques of mime, M. Lecoq explained and demonstrated various masks developed by the Commedia dell'Arte, and by himself. In the final lecture-performance, under the title "From Sight to Sound", Leon Kirchner, discussed some of the factors that affect the interpretation of music. Points were demonstrated by Kirchner at the piano and by a small chamber group.

The events, all free to the public, were scheduled toward the middle of each semester and publicized throughout the university and the city of Cambridge, though the primary audience is the staff and students at the Harvard Graduate School of Education who plan to enter secondary school teaching and administrative careers. Attendance has ranged from 250 to more than 1100 with approximately half of each audience coming from the School of Education. The setting for the presentations is generally a university lecture room with a low platform and stations for audiovisual equipment. Most programs are approximately two hours long, with a brief intermission and refreshments served afterward. All include opportunity for the audience to question the artist during or after the event.

As the title "Art in the Making" suggests, the Project's concern is to reveal something of the artist's way of working, not just to display and explicate his products. Each event unveils patterns of dealing with artistic problems rarely seen in public: the exploration of alternatives, the meeting of constraints imposed by different media, the constant reworking in search of the right effect. The programs stress that the artist continually perceives, compares, and selects among options, and that a completed work is generally achieved choice by choice, rather than in one burst of inspiration.

Our aim is not to put the artist on display or to teach members of the audience how to become artists, but to increase their sensitivity and discrimination, to encourage inquisitive looking and listening, to induce the experience of perceiving works and a world anew. Becoming acquainted with some of the decisions an artist makes, and factors he takes into consideration, may sometimes reveal aspects of a work and an art that many in the audience had never before discerned.

At its best, this effect is subtle and rare, a goal always sought, occasionally approached, but seldom fully achieved. The Project marshals a variety of means to encourage rapport. The artists invited are carefully chosen not only for the merit of their work but for their openness and their sense of pace and showmanship. Questions and comments are invited both during and after the presentation. The artist is informed of, and encouraged to tailor his program to, the sophistication of the expected audience. In addition, the artist is invited to a meeting with members of the Project's basic research staff where an outline of the presentation is discussed. Often the artist's plan has been altered somewhat in response to inquiries and comments by Project members and a more revealing lecture-performance has resulted. And "Art in the Making" has provided a laboratory for informal experimentation in arts education.

Although the Project could not continue this particular program after the first four years, the *Learning from Performers* program now conducted by the Office for the Arts at Harvard is a lively descendant.

Education for Arts Management

That the skills of the producer are essential to production in many of the arts is a truth as neglected as it is obvious. In theater and opera—and in music and dance when many performers are involved—organization, personnel management, promotion, sales, accounting, financing, and other business functions are means not merely of marketing finished work but of making it possible. These arts require coordination of many people, money, housing, and an audience. And even if the poet and painter can work alone, the effect of the publisher and dealer on production are by no means negligible. Museum management, also, can do more than acquire, preserve, and display works of art; it can use them to develop understanding and (unless distracted by pressure to give the artist direct support) to educate an audience for the artist.

Project Zero has recognized from the beginning the vital importance of management in the arts, but was unable for some time to do anything toward improvement of education in this field. Then Thomas Crooks, director of the Harvard University Summer School, asked us for ideas for summer programs in arts education. We suggested introducing a course in arts management. As a result, a committee was formed, and a valuable supply of relevant case material was made available by professors in the Harvard Business School faculty.

We finally settled on a four-week, full-time, intensive Institute, beginning in the summer of 1970, with a faculty consisting mainly of members of the Business School. The Institute has been attended by junior and senior people actively engaged in various aspects of management of orchestras, opera and dance companies, museums, arts centers, arts councils, etc., as well as by students and prospective managers.

In addition to making the initial suggestion, the director of Project Zero was a member of the planning committee and was on the faculty for the first year. He and Howard Gardner also prepared a case study on the question of museum admission fees; and this study was used to introduce discussion of fundamental issues concerning the goals and functions of museums. Through a compilation of excerpts from various museum reports from many different years, attention was again focused on implicit and explicit aims and on the relative weight given to acquisition, conservation, scholarship, exhibition, entertainment, and education.

Still badly needed is more study of those aspects of arts management that are peculiar to production in the arts: ways of selecting directors, performers, companies; special problems of working with artists; maintenance of artistic standards under severe practical difficulties; means of developing sensitivity and interest in the prospective audience; selection among or integration of several objectives—superior productions, development of the art and of artists, education of the public, and survival. The baffling problem of how to foster such skills urgently needs study.

The Problem of Evaluation

Theory

How is a method or program of education in the arts to be judged? This perplexing problem haunts our study at every step, for if we know what we are doing, we ought to know how to tell whether we are making progress toward our goal.

Some of the troubles here are common to other research in education: the long time between a course of education and its eventual results; the difficulty of distinguishing the effects of the education from those of countless other intermingled factors; the near impossibility of maintaining nearly adequate experimental controls. With arts education, though, the problem of evaluation is gravely aggravated by two further factors.

The first consists of prevalent confusion about, vacillation among, and intermixing of goals. Although the natural first question in attempting to evaluate a given program is "What is the objective?", few of those who ask for evaluations are prepared to answer unequivocally, and some even resent the question. Examination often reveals a tangle of incongruous aims: providing means of recreation or escape, development of personality, spiritual or moral uplift, social elevation, improvement of practical skills, etc. But while this confusion troubles the evaluator in the field, we cut through it so far as our research goes by setting as our goal the improvement of production and comprehension of works of art. If pursuit of this goal conflicts with realization of others, the choice among or balancing of goals is not our concern. Our problem of evaluation is solely that of judging effectiveness with respect to this one goal.

The statement of our goal only underlines, however, the second and chilling difficulty: if improved production means production of better or of more good works of art, by what standards are works to be judged? When the problem is not ignored by educators, it is usually answered in one of a number of unsatisfactory ways. Sometimes one particular set of canons is explicitly or tacitly accepted, with no recognition of the variability and dynamism of standards of aesthetic merit. Sometimes the matter is vaguely referred to "experts", ignoring ubiquitous disagreement among experts and the fact that with respect to current and developing art, judging an expert is as hard as judging a work. Unless we are reconciled to programs of art education designed to perpetuate the status quo at a particular place and time, unless we are ready to accept as ultimate a program of education that produces generations of summer resort painters, we have to find a better answer.

In reaction against provincialism and absolutism, sheer innovation has sometimes been taken as the criterion of merit; but obviously mere departure from local and transient standards has little more to recommend it than does conformity to them.

The temptation is to resign the problem and leave the appraisal of a program and of works to the sensitivity, taste, and judgment of the individual director. These qualities are invaluable; but to leave the matter there is to abandon all search for any general communicable principles that can guide and supplement—and aid us in judging—such appraisals.

On second thought, we may notice that the judgment of scientific theories is beset by much the same problems as judgments of works of art. Conceptions of admissible method and of acceptable basic concepts change, gradually or suddenly. Lead-ing experts disagree with each other and with their own earlier views. And even a satisfactory theoretical definition of scientific truth or aesthetic merit would provide no ready judgments of particular theories or works.

Nevertheless, we are faced with the nasty question how to validate research into arts education or test conclusions without ready and reliable rules for measuring artistic value. An impor-tant part of the answer is that we must judge educational ideas and programs less in the light of aesthetic standards applied to the ultimate results than in the light of what we can discover concerning the functioning of human beings, the nature of the processes involved in various phases of the production and un-derstanding of works in the several arts, and ways of fostering abilities to carry out those processes. If we can judge compara-tive effectiveness of equipment designed to operate on Mars, with no opportunity to observe actual performance, perhaps we can estimate the way various educational programs may provide means necessary for or conducive to production or understand-ing in the arts. (And to forestall an eager objection, we are *not* saying that an artist is mechanical equipment.) Thus the criteria for evaluating educational programs will evolve as research pro-ceeds and knowledge of relevant factors increases. But this an-swer calls for a good deal of explanation and defense.

The central notion here is that we bypass the question of aes-thetic standards by focusing upon those abilities that are neces-sary or conducive to production or comprehension in the arts. Certain skills are required for riding a bicycle—whether riding well or badly; a dancer, good or bad, has to be able to execute certain movements; and so on. Mastery of the component skills surely does not imply being a good bicycle rider or a good dancer; and just for that reason, to forego judgment of overall performance or ultimate result is not to forego judgment of im-provement in component skills. An important consideration here is that much of the disagreement about aesthetic standards leaves untouched considerable agreement about abilities to perform processes essential to artistic production. To oversimplify (almost to caricature) the point, those who disagree about whether a student can paint well or draw well may agree entirely as to whether he can draw a circle well. This to some extent explains the emphasis in our research on the nature of problem-solving in the arts. Skill in working sample problems in art or science is not sufficient for superior performance but is an indication of progress.

The reader will naturally object that the virtues of this approach arise from and throw into relief its fatal defect. For if judgment of success in performing sample exercises and mastering component skills does not imply judgment of overall performance, that is just because these component abilities by no means ensure superior overall performance; and there is thus no guarantee that an educational program that improves these component skills will result in better production or understanding. Here again a comparison with science is helpful. What scientific education does, for the most part, is to provide the means needed and helpful for scientific work. The ability to do arithmetic, to perform simple experiments, to carry out logical arguments, will not make a great or original physicist, but one can hardly become a superior physicist without these accomplishments. Had science education focused exclusively on developing the creative scientist, or finding and nurturing the genius, it would be in as sorry a state as is art education today. Throughout our work we have subordinated the usual concentration upon "creativity" to consideration of ways of providing means. Possession of requisite or conducive skills makes possible superior performance by those capable of it.

Some of our examples may have given the false impression that we are concerned only with such simple skills as drawing geometric figures, playing scales, or (in science) doing arithmetic. But just as training in science involves developing also such more complex skills as performing quantitative chemical analyses, developing promising hypotheses, and designing crucial experiments, so must education for the arts involve developing such skills as making fine perceptual discriminations, grasping elusive relationships, discerning obscure patterns. An artist cannot work with what he cannot detect. Which skills are more important—indeed, which skills are needed at all—may vary with the art and the phase of artisitic production or comprehension in question, with style or school or doctrine, and with the individual artist; for instance, subtlety of sensory discrimination rates low for many contemporary artists but high for many earlier schools. The educator is concerned with how to develop relevant skills, leaving to others the comparative emphasis upon or choice among them. But, of course, he must still decide what skills are most likely to be relevant.

Yet one may ask whether in the training for understanding, if not for production, standards of taste will not have to be imparted. The answer is complex. In the first place, any attempt to indoctrinate any standards as absolute and universal is indefensible. A reading of the damning comments, by critics of their time, on Rembrandt or Brahms or many others among the greatest figures in the arts should destroy any confidence in current evaluation of contemporary work. Moreover, "Gothic" and "primitive" were once widely accepted terms of opprobrium. On the other hand, expert judgment of the comparative merit of works within (but not across) the production of a particular well-known earlier school or artist are more useful. Training in these judgments and how they are made may improve understanding in two ways. First, responsible judgments of merit often serve as incitement to discover differences that had gone completely unnoticed (*LA* VI,6); thus aesthetic evaluation serves as a prelude to rather than the goal of deeper understanding. Second, exposure to critical judgments within different schools or cultures or by different artists may make the student aware of alternatives to whatever standards have imprisoned him, without giving him the impression that quality does not matter.

Thus the educator or the investigator of education in the arts need neither adopt any absolute aesthetic standards nor abandon all hope of evaluating his own work.

Practice

The consultant in the field, faced with the task of evaluating educational ideas, programs, and methods, will not find in our theoretical analysis a prescription for just how to proceed. His normal first step will be to try to determine the acknowledged objective; and to attempt an evaluation only insofar as that objective is improvement of production and understanding in the arts. Then, or concurrently, he will survey the situation with all the knowledge, sensitivity, taste, and good judgment at his command. Despite our strictures against applying any aesthetic standards as absolute, he will not hesitate to make his own judgment on the quality of any work produced. (And incidentally, judgments that particular works produced within given restrictions are bad have a comparatively high degree of reliability.)

This initial informal appraisal he will take as a preliminary to a more systematic investigation. He will use a theoretical analysis, such as we have set forth above, in testing his judgments, in probing beneath and beyond them, in asking himself critical questions. To what extent is the quality of work immediately produced a measure of the success of this particular program? Does the program have, or should it consider having, the training of skills toward future production or eventual understanding as its major goal? What skills are most needed for the art or phase of art in question? How effective are the methods used for developing such skills? Are some more important skills overlooked? What alternatives may be suggested in formulation of goal, in choice or balancing of component factors?

In particular, the evaluator will also try to differentiate between those virtues and defects that do and those that do not depend primarily on the particular people involved in the program. The gifted educator in any field is an irreplaceable asset, and the inept educator a heavy liability. But the personnel in almost any program changes frequently; and the evaluator's primary concern is with measures that may maximize the good educator's effectiveness and minimize the poor one's shortcomings.

Judgment of success or failure is the beginning rather than the end of the evaluator's responsibility. What he should provide are suggestions for making improvements; for correcting deficiencies and strengthening virtues of the program. And he will keep in mind the thought—chastening or comforting—that a poor program may sometimes be better than none.

3. A MESSAGE FROM MARS

Professor Hans Trublemacher, a noted specialist in science education, was recently called to Mars as a consultant at the request of Martians who were concerned about the state of the sciences at the major university on the planet. A letter describing his experiences follows.

I was greeted warmly on arrival by Chancellor Eric Cobb, who told me that the improvement of science education at the University was one of his primary interests. He felt no student could have a rounded education without some exposure to the sciences, that some acquaintance with the sciences would improve the quality of mind and personality and increase the skill of statesmen, lawyers, artists, and other pillars of Martian civilization. Furthermore, since working hours on Mars were being rapidly shortened and early retirement encouraged, everyone should have some familiarity with and a proficiency in the sciences to occupy leisure time. And he decried the ascetic tradition that looked down on the sciences merely because they could provide pleasure and satisfaction. But funding presented great problems.

In the first few days of my visit I found that the official courses at the University here focus almost entirely on the arts, covering all their aspects. A wide variety of undergraduate and graduate degree programs in the arts were offered for students who would become creative or performing artists or members of the audiences for the several arts. The University maintained companies of professional actors, mimes, dancers, and musicians, and the faculty comprised many composers, painters, sculptors, poets, playwrights, architects, and choreographers, some occupied partly in teaching or training, others engaged solely in their own work. There were adequate theaters, concert halls, studios of all sorts, museums, and expert technical staffs.

In contrast, the only science courses in the catalog were in the history of science, and technological courses supporting one aspect or another of work in the arts such as chemistry of pigments, electronics for the stage, photographic optics, conservation. There were no courses in any of the sciences as we know them, no program of undergraduate or graduate study in any science, and no laboratory work or facilities for it except in the technologies mentioned.

After my preliminary survey, I had a conference with former Dean Christopher Chrysler. When I remarked that the title "Dean of Sciences and Arts" seemed somewhat anomalous when the sciences played so subsidiary a role in the University, he said that he had heard that his counterpart at Harvard had the title "Dean of Arts and Sciences." He expressed himself, nevertheless, as favorably disposed to the sciences. When I asked about what seemed to me an utterly rudimentary program in the sciences as compared to the arts, he pointed out that I had so far looked only at the official courses and activities, and that I would have a different view of the whole situation when I observed all that was going on in the sciences on an extracurricular basis. The Dean was proud of the intensive and varied activities in the sciences that students were carrying on, and did his best to encourage them with the limited money available. Furthermore, he felt it best for the sciences at the University that they should not be subject to the constraints of formal programs, that the faculty was firmly convinced that the intrusion of the sciences into the credit programs would lower standards, that scientific genius and proficiency could not be developed by formal education or evaluated on the same basis as work in the art program of the university; and finally, that students were so fascinated by and devoted to their scientific projects that there was no need for courses, grades, credit, or official recognition. He also doubted whether a truly creative scientist could flourish in the atmosphere of the University, and felt that to master a science would leave a student inadequate time for any of the regular work of the University. He suggested that I talk with Professor Lawrence Vincent, who had been for many years faculty supervisor of the Sciences Club and the administration's trusted advisor on the sciences.

During the next few days I was indeed much impressed by the quantity and variety of the extracurricular activities in the sciences. In the communes comprising the student body there were various clubs: chemistry clubs, biology clubs, physics clubs, astronomy clubs, astrology clubs, numerology clubs, etc. There was a prominent and venerable club devoted to the study of William Gilbert's experiments on magnetism and Robert Boyle's experiments on gases; and this Gilbert and Boyle Society performed some of these experiments to the delight of large audiences each year. In some of the communes, there were open evenings, when students brought in their own equipment and repeated famous experiments. There was one large and well equipped laboratory primarily for student use and subsidized by the University, but dominated by the rather pedestrian Sciences Club. However, in the dormitories of the communes, the kitchens after dinner were often turned into improvised laboratories, and some of the most popular presentations occurred there.

Moreover, famous scientists were brought to the University for as much as two or three days at a time, so that students could see them at work. And just recently some of the technical staff that assisted the work of the Sciences Club were giving special noncredit courses; for example, a two-week course in chemistry, a three-week 'comprehensive' course in modern physics, and six lectures on metallurgy.

The only case where a course in science was being given for credit resulted from a subterfuge by a distinguished pianist and Professor of Music who felt that some work in pure mathematics would be a welcome change from the pervasive emphasis on composition and performance. He surreptitiously introduced a course in modern algebra under the title "Mathematical Aspects of the Performance of Groups."

I next inquired into the extensive efforts the administration was reputedly making to better the state of the sciences at the University. A survey report had been commissioned and received after about two years. After serious consideration of the report for a year or so more, a Council on the Sciences was appointed, which after another year came up with one specific recommendation. This, however, immediately proved unfeasible and was dropped in favor of a quickly devised substitute.

An Office of the Sciences was established, and a Coordinator for the Sciences appointed. I asked the Coordinator, Mr. Paul Purchance, about the function of the Office and about his own work. He explained his efforts to bring some order out of the chaos. A shortage of scientific equipment was being made less of a handicap by proper planning and distribution, so that not everyone would be calling for test tubes at the same time. The limited laboratory space was sometimes in demand by several groups, and at other times lay idle. Furthermore, several experiments and demonstrations were sometimes scheduled on the same day; and this was especially bad when four different groups on campus decided to experiment, on the same evening, in producing noxious gases. The Coordinator was helping to plan schedules; and also was administering a new program for sending students to outside teachers for lessons in chemistry and physics. All these efforts, though useful, were somewhat peripheral; the Coordinator was seriously handicapped by having also been saddled with the considerable and incompatible job of running some of the extracurricular science programs himself.

I talked, finally, with Professor Lawrence Vincent, a faculty member who had long been powerful in forming and directing the science activities at the University. He emphasized the fact that the University was constantly under financial pressure and could not attempt to do everything. The real business of the University was education in all aspects of the arts. Scientific training he regarded as primarily vocational, and better left to trade schools. Furthermore, science insofar as it was not technology was a somewhat idle pursuit, having entertainment value only; and scientific activities, like athletic activities at the University, should be kept apart from the regular curriculum. The proper role of physics, he felt, was very much like that of football. He rejected completely any suggestion that the University might maintain research laboratories and scientists engaged primarily in research for much the same reason that it maintained theaters and professional companies and artists.

The friend who had invited me to come as consultant asked me, on a drive to the space-port, for my impressions and recommendations. I had to tell him I thought that little could be done until there was more recognition of the basic need for a change in attitude, and that new ideas were needed more than, or at least before, new money. He suggested trading his university for Harvard; but I was eager to return home where the importance of the sciences is recognized and the arts are kept in their proper place.

4. ART AND IDEAS

Museum directors, more than other people, ought to think hard and often about what they are doing and why. Most don't. Sherman Lee does; and some results are to be seen in the superb Cleveland Museum of Art, which he has directed for twenty-five years, and in some penetrating papers. Both by example and by argument, he has made his views on museums so clear and convincing that nothing more is needed to strengthen his case or would be likely to lessen the widespread and stubborn opposition to it.

Underlying his views is a deep and constant concern with the interrelationship between art and ideas. Here he has had to overcome the drawback of being both a museum director and an art historian; for museums and art history often frown on intercourse between art and ideas. Lee insists that they belong together and examines how they should interact.

That is not easy. In a key passage, he writes:

The art museum is not fundamentally concerned with therapy, illustrating history, social action, entertainment or scientific research . . . The museum . . . is a *primary source* of wonder and delight for mind and heart. In this, the art museum is comparable to a permanent storage battery, or to a library of original manuscripts.[7]

The accent on delight might be taken as an endorsement of what I have called the Tingle-Immersion theory of art were the delight not specified to be of the *mind* as well as of the heart or were the

7. "Art Museums and Education", cited in note 2 above. This and all other papers by Sherman Lee mentioned in this section appear in *Past, Present, East and West* (New York: George Braziller, 1983).

art museum not so improbably compared both to a battery and to a library of manuscripts. Here Lee, after stressing what a museum is not, uses startling similes to suggest what a museum is.

Later he zeroes in on a virulent confusion. So long as education is taken to be entirely verbal, the main function of a museum is not educational; but in the "world of visual images", he contends, the museum is the chief instrument of education; and "the original worth of visual images" must be "re-incorporated into a basic concept of education as the transmission of *all* knowledge." We cannot tolerate "the submission of vision to literacy".

Education plainly cannot be exclusively verbal in either its ends or its means; for it consists not merely of adding to knowledge—to true beliefs—but of the overall advancement of understanding. And understanding a painting, for example, involves discerning its special stylistic and other visual properties—learning how to see it and to see in terms of it. Such learning is as inquisitive, as cognitive a process as grasping a mathematical theorem or a scientific concept, but it cannot be reduced to or induced by words alone. It requires accessibility of works, pointed juxtapositions for comparison and contrast, everything that encourages hard looking and aids intelligent seeing. That includes words; for words may illuminate pictures as pictures may illuminate words. Neither the verbal nor the nonverbal gives way to the other; they participate together in the growth of understanding, and interact as equals.

Just this conviction that art is not for passive absorption but for active visual inquiry, that understanding pictures means grasping ideas (albeit nonverbal ideas), and that painting and literature and science are allies rather than enemies might have been partly responsible for Sherman Lee's special interest in Oriental art. For in the first place, the Westerner usually finds that with Oriental works his problem of understanding is more insistently present and his processes thus more open to observation than with most works of his own culture. In the second place, the Orient has a venerable tradition of intimate association among artists and writers and scholars, among painting and poetry and learning and thinking of all kinds. And one might conjecture that Sherman Lee's lack of interest in American Indian and other primitive arts may be partly due to their having no such background, though he would surely agree that they likewise demand thoughtful seeing.

Sherman Lee's papers stimulate, inform, enlighten, and sometimes startle. On reading that Japanese art exaggerates some features of Chinese art, we may wonder whether such 'exaggeration' might not rather be described as a shift in emphasis prophetic of some important developments in modern Western art; but one disputes Sherman Lee with trepidation. Consider, for example, his paper on Demuth's illustrational watercolors. Written at the age of twenty-four, this perceptive and thorough study must have impressed the establishment of art historians, but it must have shocked many of them by the opening pronouncement that Marin and Demuth are the greatest American watercolorists—a fair enough judgment now but hardly orthodox in 1942. In those days you could get a basketful of Demuths for a single Homer.

The Cleveland Museum and these essays on various arts serve surpassingly well their common end: to better the understanding of the works in question, to make these works work.

5. THE END OF THE MUSEUM?

As a long-time addict of the arts, an intemperate collector, and an inveterate museum-goer, I could not summon enough discretion to decline an invitation to give the keynote address at an annual meeting of the Association of American Museums. So with only the lesser part of valor, I risked what follows.

Questions

I share your wonderment that experts from institutions concerned with everything from penguins to periscopes and from peonies to Piero della Francescas should be asked to listen to a philosopher ignorant of all these matters. Some of you will expect me to solve all the most profound capital-letter problems of

Life, Values, and Human Destiny, while the rest of you are firmly convinced that a philosopher knows nothing of any use to anybody. This second group is the nearer right.

A philosopher, indeed, knows nothing. Accordingly he tries to find out something by asking everyone questions. What I am supposed to do here, I take it, it to distract you for a time from worries about budget gaps, striking guards, stubborn trustees, and new laboratory reports on your most prized masterpieces, by raising annoying questions about what in the world you are trying to do and why. Socrates held that those he questioned knew all about everything but had temporarily forgotten it. And I am likewise sure that I can learn the answers to these questions from you if I bother you enough. I must say, though, that I am somewhat unnerved by the reflection that in the end what Socrates got for his trouble was a cup of poison.

I shall be focusing upon art museums because I am most familiar with them, because attempting complete generality throughout would result in diffuseness, and because art museums present most acutely many of the problems common to all museums. However, I shall later suggest why art museums are not so different from others as is usually supposed, and in the meantime, I hope that as I go on you will often see an application to your own institution, of whatever type.

Museums and Other Houses

Perhaps the first impression one gets from some museums and some writing about museums is that a museum functions much like such other institutions as a house of detention, a house of rehabilitation, or a house of pleasure; or in the vernacular, a jailhouse, a madhouse, or—a teahouse. I am sure you have had days when your own museum seemed like one of these, or even like all three combined.

These comparisons are not altogether facetious. A museum may maintain an elaborate intelligence network to capture the wanted, and a security system to prevent their escape or to protect vulnerable inmates. And by overwhelming popular opinion supported by a distressing number of official statements, a primary function of the museum is to provide the opportunity for a few moments of inconsequent pleasure.

Sometimes, again, the behavior and reports of a museum suggest rather that it is like a professional ball park, where what counts is how many people go through the gates. On the other hand, is it perhaps possible that a museum may be more like a hospital, where what matters is not how many patients enter, but what happens to them while they are there?

To these hit-and-run remarks, let me add a final, somewhat more detailed comparison. A few years ago an old friend of mine, Professor Hans Trublemacher, visited Mars and wrote a report (see V,3 above) on the sad state of science education there, where, it seems, in many leading institutions education in the sciences is entirely extracurricular and is treated in much the same way as education in the arts in many leading universities on Earth: that is, as a way of giving people something to do in their leisure time. Later, Professor Trublemacher made another trip, on the request of the Martians themselves, to evaluate their libraries. I quote from one of his letters:

Until twenty years ago, the Martians had no libraries. They sent a committee to Earth to survey our libraries here and to set up a like system on their return. But something seems to have gone astray.

In a typical Martian library there are no tables, desks, or cubicles, and seldom any chairs except for the guards. There are no open shelves, and no books circulate. In each reading room, certain of the most important books are set out on separate pedestals, against the wall and behind a rail that keeps readers about four feet away, pages being turned by remote control. Frequently, groups of children are led through the room while a docent lectures about the books. In the newer libraries several readers had electronic packets strapped on, and I discovered that these were miniature projectors, rented by the libraries, that flashed a sequence of slides just above the text in the reader's visual field. I could not determine whether the purpose was to make sure the reader had the proper images accompanying the text, or to pace his reading, or merely to give him something to occupy his mind while reading.

All in all I found very inspiring the sight of people standing and doggedly reading a book more than an arm's length away, while machines flashed pictures and docents chattered to their charges; but I could understand why the shop at the entrance was doing a brisk business selling small (and of course unreadable) plaster reproductions of some of the more popular volumes.

Now obviously the Martians, from our point of view, had somewhere gotten their antennas crossed. You can't run a library the way they run a library; and you can't run a library the way we run a museum. But the question arises whether you can run a museum the way they run a library—that is, whether you can run a museum the way we run a museum.

Of course, there are at least two obvious differences that make it impossible to run a museum as we run a library: first, that the museum's works can't be circulated or put on open shelves; and second, that while most of those who use a library know how to read, most of those who visit a museum don't know how to see. I'll come back to this later.

These brief comparisons and contrasts may by indirection and negation sidelight or backlight some aspects of what a museum is and is not. But after all you are not, except perhaps on the side, running a jail or a sanatorium or a teahouse or a superdome or a hospital or a library. You are running a museum. What can be said for this cultural curiosity, this institutional monstrosity? Well, some of what *is* said can be found in your annual reports and your appeals, in speeches by officers of arts councils and foundations, and by members of legislative and administrative organs of governments. And to most of what is said, I cry:

Deliver Us from Our Defenders

What you and others say often adds up to something like this: that museums provide a relaxed way of filling up the spare time that advancing technology has given us; that they exert a humanizing influence against the overintellectual, materialistic tenor of our times; that they reduce juvenile delinquency and, by stressing the spiritual, make for moral betterment of citizens and community; and that museums, by attracting tourists, providing jobs, and stimulating the expanding art market, contribute to prosperity.

The case put more or less in these terms has become so familiar that we often forget how hollow it is. All these arguments, of course, are beside the point, and some are simply false. Museums, like theaters, sometimes do provide pleasure for leisure, but what have exhibitions of Goya's *Disasters of War* or Picasso's *Guernica* to do with pleasure? To contend that museums foster our humanity in the face of current intellectual and scientific fervor suggests that what museums do is not intellectual, and that scientific activity is not human. As for moral uplift, there is equal evidence that museums offer outstanding opportunities for vandalism, and promote cupidity and connivance. The only moral effect a museum has on me is a temptation to rob the place. And while museums do attract tourists and stimulate cash flow, that is done better by gambling casinos.

Of course, your arguments are designed for those you must convince: foundations, politicians, chambers of commerce, trustees, and the public. You will hardly be misled yourself by the specious challenge to justify museums in terms of what they, on the contrary, help to justify. Shakespeare's plays and Bach's music—and Einstein's theorems, too—can give pleasure, occupy leisure, elevate character, and contribute to the economy, but quite plainly, that is not the point. The pleasure is incidental. The point of having leisure time, of a decent moral climate, of prosperity beyond basic need, lies in what these can help make possible. The plays, the music, the mathematical physics, and painting and sculpture do not pose the question "why?"; they answer it. To look at it the opposite way is to demean your profession and your institution.

The Museum's Mission

You will have gathered by now that, despite some irreverence, I am thoroughly convinced of the high importance of the museum's mission. What is that mission? We have come closest to it, I think, in the comparison with libraries. Libraries and museums alike collect and preserve works and make them available for public use. Library and museum staffs thus have in their charge enormously powerful agents for transforming ourselves and our environment. Libraries and museums alike are fundamentally educational rather than recreational institutions.

But we noticed that museums face problems that libraries do not: first, while most users of a library know how to read the books there, many visitors to a museum do not know how to see, or to see in terms of, the works there; and second, the works in a museum must be viewed under severe and stultifying restraints. Unless the museum, despite its handicaps, finds ways of inculcating the ability to see and of aiding and abetting the exercise of that ability, the other functions of the museum will be pointless and its works as dormant as books in an unreadable language or in locked bindings. The museum has to function as an institution for the prevention and cure of blindness in order to make works work. And making works work is the museum's major mission.

That raises four questions. What, more expressly, does it mean for works to work? What are the special obstacles to be surmounted or circumvented? How, despite the obstacles, can works be made to work? And how can you judge the success of your efforts to make them work?

The Work of Works

What we see in a museum may profoundly affect what we see when we leave; and this is as true for nonrepresentational as for representational works. Our worlds are no less powerfully informed by the patterns and feelings of abstract works than by a literal Chardin still-life or an allegorical "Birth of Venus". In the words of *Ways of Worldmaking* (VI,5), "After we spend an hour or so at one or another exhibition of abstract painting, everything tends to square off into geometric patches or swirl in circles or weave into textural arabesques, to sharpen into black and white or vibrate with new color consonances and dissonances". In turn, what we see when we leave the museum may appreciably affect what we see when we return.

Works work when by stimulating inquisitive looking, sharpening perception, raising visual intelligence, widening perspectives, bringing out new connections and contrasts, and marking off neglected significant kinds, they participate in the organization and reorganization of experience, and thus in the making and remaking of our worlds. If that sounds grandiloquent, I must insist that I am not romanticizing or rhapsodizing here, not talking of ecstasy or rapture or the miraculous or the visionary, but calling attention to down-to-earth facts abundantly attested by observation, by able writers on art, and by psychological experiment. The myths of the innocent eye, the insular intellect, the mindless emotion, are obsolete. Sensation and perception and feeling and reason are all facets of cognition, and they affect and are affected by each other. Works work when they inform vision; *inform* not by supplying information but by *forming* or *re*-forming or *trans*forming vision; vision not as confined to ocular perception but as understanding in general. Clearly, works of science work in this sense, too, and so also do the collections of museums of science and museums of cultural and natural history, as well as the collections of botanical and zoological gardens and of all the institutions that make up this Association. The differences between the arts and the sciences have been, I think, misunderstood and overstressed; outmoded dichotomies have contrasted them in misleading ways and even engendered antagonisms. Museums of different kinds do have some different problems, but their common end is improvement in the comprehension and creation of the worlds we live in.

But a work must not be treated as a mere visual aid for use in seeing what lies beyond it. Equally important is how we see the work, and what we see in it, in terms of a world we build partly in terms of the work. Reverberations from a work may travel in cycles through our everyday environment, other works, and itself, again and again, with ever-changing effect. Works work by interacting with all our experience and all our cognitive processes in the continuing advancement of our understanding.

Obstacles

Even the most able work, however, does not always work. Whether it does or not will depend also upon the capacities and condition of the viewer, and the surroundings and circumstances of the viewing. The museum has to contend with inexperience and ineptness in many viewers, a fixed and formidable environment for viewing, and usually with lack of any mobility or progression or time-value in the work itself. Before we consider what measures may be taken, let me expand briefly on these obstacles.

First, as I have already insisted, what we see in a work and what we take from it depends heavily on what we bring to it: upon relevant experience and skills involved in our looking— upon pertinent visual inquiry. The museum cannot instantly supply the needed experience and competence but must find ways of fostering their acquisition. Audience development is not finished when lines form at the door.

Second, the circumstances for viewing in a museum are at best abnormal and adverse. The viewer cannot handle a work, try it in different lights, put it beside various other works for comparison, take it home, come upon it in a sunbeam reflected from snow, contemplate it in comfort. The floors in a museum will defeat any feet and wrack any back; the distance from turnstile to object you want to see is longer than from airport entrance to your flight; the displays are as if congealed in a glass paperweight, the lighting as unvarying as in summer at the Poles, the oases as scarce as in Death Valley, and the atmosphere as bristling with prohibitions as in the Pentagon. All this occasions some rather ludicrous behavior. If you thought my comparison of a museum to a home for the mentally deranged far-fetched, where except in these two institutions do you expect to find anyone standing stock-still staring at a wall where nothing is going on? Our justifiable concern over the cost and rarity of works, and the need to protect them from theft and violence and deterioration, have reinforced the inherent tendency of the museum to become a place hostile to the achievement of its own main purpose.

Third, and aggravating the other difficulties, is the timeless-ness of most works in a museum. Unlike a play or a concert, a painting or sculpture is all there at once. And although a book, too, is all there at once, you start reading on the first page and stop when you reach the last. You can go back if you like, but the difference between going back and going forward is clear. But where do you start and when do you stop looking at a picture? There is no going forward or backward, no beginning and no end. You can take it all in, superficially, at a glance, and the aver-age looking time per viewer per picture viewed must be some-thing under five seconds. Dynamic as a work may be in expression and design, it is physically inert, while the human being is alive and restless. Psychologists have found that what is looked at by the unmoving eye tends to fade out; that change is essential to perception. Somehow, the immutable work and the volatile viewer have to be reconciled. Attention must be held long enough for a work to work.

In sum, your job is to make works work under the worst imaginable conditions—that is, in a museum.

Means and Methods

How, now, can these obstacles described and others be removed, surmounted, neutralized, or evaded? Surely it is not for me, a layman, to tell you, the experts, how to solve problems that you face every day. All I can do is review for your consideration some of the issues, arguments, and possibilities.

On the question of how the viewer can be helped, there are opposing policies. The first is to show a work properly and get out of the way. Keep it free from all encumbrances, all gimmicks, all jabber. Show it well-spaced from other works, with minimal labels and nothing else. The extreme example of this is showing a work in a separate and otherwise empty gallery.

The case for such a policy is strong:

Supplementary material, whether presented by lengthy labels, gallery talks, or cinema sideshows may distract and mislead, may block the insight a viewer could gain from undisturbed study of the work itself. Where nonverbal works are concerned, words are intrusive and nonverbal aids are presumptuous and competitive. In the museum, there should be a direct, unchanneled transaction between viewer and work. One learns to see, not by being told or shown how to look, but by looking. If the viewer will try, and the work is good enough, it will work without help.

The opposite policy is to make available all sorts of help: informative and suggestive labels, pointed juxtapositions in installation, easily accessible photographs and books, live or recorded talks, film and videotapes in adjacent cubicles, and whatever else may hold and guide attention.

The case for this policy is also very strong. Against the director or curator who advocates showing a work in splendid isolation, the argument begins:

After all, that's not the way you look at a work yourself. You immediately assemble photographs of related works, consult books and articles, see all the comparable works possible (even taking the trouble to visit Europe on a grant), and generally betray your proclaimed principle that all there is in a work can be seen by looking at it apart from all else. If with your experience and skill, you still need informative and comparative material before you, how can you expect the novice and the amateur to do without it? As for the idea that words are an intrusion where nonverbal works are concerned, we need only remember how comment by a Meyer Schapiro[8] can illuminate Cézanne's "Bather". But the development of discrimination requires also presentation by example of some of the subtle differences and covert kinships between works. Much of the looking we learn by is comparative looking. What can be found in a work is intimately involved with other works seen, and with other experience. As no man is an island, neither is any work.

In the face of this conflict between the two policies, what shall we do? Seek further arguments for whichever position we favor? Or compromise? Or vacillate? More to the point, in view of the virtues and vices of each policy—in view of the danger that proffered help may distract and that lack of help may leave the

8. Meyer Schapiro, *Cézanne* (New York: Harry N. Abrams, 1952), pp. 68–69.

looker lost—what particular means and measures shall we choose?

For dealing with the artificial and uncomfortable conditions for viewing works in a museum, we seem to be restricted to such needed but inadequate measures as carpeting, seating, daylight when possible, and demilitarization of the guards. Security and conservation cannot be sacrificed; we cannot give the viewer free access to the works or lend them to him. What we have to do, therefore, is to find other means of extending the museum's influence beyond the museum building into the more natural setting—of homes and working places.

The commonest device, though often thought of more as a source of revenue than as an educational instrument, is the shop or sales desk. The visitor's experience in the museum can to some extent be prolonged and enhanced if he can take away photographs, even postcards, and pertinent books. They serve as reminders of what he has seen. The sale of plaster reproductions is much more controversial. The argument for them is that they are substitutes for the originals since the amateur cannot tell the difference, and that they are inexpensive enough to be thrown away when he comes to know better. The contrary view holds that the ready disposability of these imitations is their best feature.

For how can the person with a daily visual diet at home consisting of imitations that lack most of the important qualities of the original ever come to know better? How can discrimination develop when the significant subtle qualities of the genuine works are missing? We might do better to install the imitations beside the originals, where the differences can be seen.

A less frequent response to the problem is the sales and rental gallery where original works can be found to take home. These are not, indeed, the present masterpieces in the museum's collection; but the visitor fresh from seeing those can here apply his newfound excitement and acuity to choosing a work to live with. Surely for the present audience I need not dwell on the enormous growth in understanding that can result from so intimate an acquaintanceship, whether the work wears well or wilts.

When the visitor to the museum is motivated to rent or buy an original work, the museum is making its own works work beyond its walls. 'The museum without walls' in my view embraces not reproductions but a wider range of genuine works.

But the sales and rental gallery, and the sales exhibition, may be resisted on the ground that the museum thus dirties its hands with commerce and opens its doors to works of lesser quality, or at least of less well-recognized quality, than those in its collection. Here, I am afraid the evil side of elitism looms. Insistence on excellence in works for the museum, and refusal of all compromise with popular taste, are all to the good; for the muscles of the mind must stretch to be strengthened. But giving the impression that the only works worthwhile are those so rare and costly as to be confined to museums and great collections, that there are no good works that people can own and live with—this is one of the worst effects a museum can have. And when works begin to be produced expressly for museums, we reach a stage of utter perversity. For the museum after all is an anomalous and awkward institution made necessary only by the rarity and vulnerability of works that belong elsewhere.

On the problem presented by the timelessness of works— their being all there all the time—I can be very brief; for many of the means used to help the inexpert viewer may also serve to lengthen looking time. The value of a gallery talk, for instance, may often lie less in the imparting of information than in the focusing of attention upon a work. But a more effective means may be to initiate inquiry. I suspect that children may not benefit so much from what a teacher tries to tell them in a gallery as, say, from being asked to search the gallery for another work by the same artist as an indicated work. The active inquiry that begins then and continues to a conclusion or a conjecture may well have more effect than does passive gazing. (Incidentally, some interesting research has been done recently on the age when children are first able to relate works by style rather than subject.)[9]

9. See Howard Gardner, "Style Sensitivity in Children", in *Human Development* 15 (1972) 325–338.

Signs of Success

Finally, how are you to make your decisions concerning principles, policies, and practices, and how can you tell whether you are accomplishing your purpose? Lists of acquisitions, accounts of donations, attendance records, columns of publicity, and number of wings the building has sprouted, speak only of means. But are you making works work?

Unfortunately, there are no crisp and clear tests. There are only signs. As a hospital's success may be gauged by improvement in the physiological and psychological health of its patients and its community, so a museum's success might be judged by the cultural health of its visitors and its community. But cultural health is much less easily judged than organic health. Again, there are only signs, signs that you may seek by asking whether people are buying original works, whether commercial galleries are surviving and what they are handling, whether serious artists are becoming recognized by the public. But the answers are not easy to arrive at and the criteria applied are debatable.

Are you, then, left with the disheartening conclusion that you never will be able to tell how well you are doing? Or can you perhaps, if not measure, at least roughly estimate your success as judged by some such criteria? Alas, even that hope may be clouded by a further problem. Consider a well-known experiment carried out a few years ago by some industrial engineers exploring ways of increasing production in factories. They spent some days in one department improving the lighting—and production immediately went up. But before they wrote into the books the law that better lighting will increase production, one of them had a second thought. He sent a crew into another department to spend some time conspicuously working on the lights but leaving them in the end exactly as they had been before—and production went up. You can predict the result of a third experiment when the lighting was made a little worse. This is the famous Hawthorne effect. (see V,n.4), also known as the Pink Pill Phenomenon, or the Doctor's Delight. Within limits, whatever you do will succeed, so long as you do, or appear to do, something. While that may sound comforting, the conclusion that improvement effected constitutes no evidence that you have been making good choices all along is, to say the least, somewhat disappointing.

Luckily, you have other resources: your own experience and the still meager and seemingly remote results of basic research. First, you yourself have been through the process—and are probably still going through the process—of learning how to look at a work, learning what helps and what hinders, and under what circumstances illumination results; and in these learning processes of your own and your colleagues you can seek guidance. Second, theoretical and laboratory research that tells us something of how human beings function in acquiring and exercising skills involved in the understanding of works can help in deciding the means and methods to be adopted in the museum. Basic research can supply no fast and full and final answers, but I am convinced that cooperation between research and practice is as much needed in making works work as in making crops grow—even though the harvest is less easily weighed.

The End

In conclusion, I have reached few conclusions. A keynote address by one who cannot sing is better called a key address and is meant not to solve anything but to unlock something. Thus I have not answered all the questions I have raised but have tried to focus your attention on them because I think that the museum's mission is as important as it is difficult, and that carrying it out successfully depends upon keeping it clearly in mind.

Appendix
Conversation with Frans Boenders and Mia Gosselin

(Revised text of a television interview conducted at the studios of the Belgian Radio-Television System in Brussels in August 1980)

FRANS BOENDERS is a Belgian critic, essayist, and poet, a writer and producer of literary and philosophical and documentary films and programs on radio and television. His programs include series on contemporary thought and culture in several Western and Eastern countries. He won the Flemish 1979 Award of Free Thought, and in 1981 his *The Hindu Pantheon*, first part of a series of six documentary films on Eastern Religions, won the First Prize awarded by the International Radio and Television University (URTI). He has written critical introductions to the catalogs of many international retrospective exhibitions of art. Currently he is Chief Producer of the Third Program of the Belgian Radio-Television system and conducts a highly successful series of interviews.

MIA GOSSELIN is Professor of Philosophy and Director of the Empiric Epistemology Center at the Free University of Brussels. Her book on nominalism in the work of Quine and Goodman will be published by Reidel. She has also written and published studies on Nietzsche, on problems in the theory of knowledge and the philosophy of science, and on the philosophy of art.

Boenders: Professor Goodman, Miss Gosselin has remarked that in all your career you have been breaking away from the narrow confines of positivism. Would you agree with that?

189

Goodman: Perhaps to some extent. Yet I certainly did not start out with the idea of breaking away from positivism. I was much attracted both by positivism's rejection of loose and abstruse metaphysical terminology and by its insistence on application of the new logical methods that were just becoming known at the time. Today few people realize what a tremendous event it was when symbolic logic burst upon the scene. It so quickly developed from a purely theoretical discovery in mathematics and logic into the enormously practical basis for all computer technology that we may forget how little time has passed since there was no such thing as symbolic logic and forget also how gratefully it was welcomed by many of us who were looking for a new aid to clarity in philosophy. On the other hand, we found some aspects of positivism inacceptable; for example, the dependence upon a distinction between analytical and synthetic judgments and the easy acceptance of a difference between so called natural and artificial kinds. We rejected some of these dogmas of empiricism, as Quine calls them, but not its spirit.

Boenders: What strikes me as an outsider is that probably since 1970 the interest in formal languages by philosophers of science has diminished. I am now thinking for example of Thomas Kuhn and Paul Feyerabend. Is this much correct—this impression I have?

Goodman: That's hard to say. Being a historian of contemporary philosophy while being in it I find very difficult. There have always been rather few people who are capable of, and who will bother with, mastering and applying the techniques of mathematical logic, and often the techniques have been applied ineptly and without worthwhile results.

Boenders: Isn't the basic question here whether we need something more than ordinary language to reconstruct the world and to make a good and, let's say, a reliable philosophy?

Goodman: I think we do, whether we use formal techniques such as symbolic logic, or simply use a vocabulary that derives from ordinary language—that begins by using terms from ordinary language and specifying ways in which the ambiguities and the vagueness of ordinary language may be resolved. Most terms in ordinary language have many uses, and if we don't notice this and try to correct it in systematic discourse, we are going to find ourselves left with all the confusions that attend our ordinary thinking.

Boenders: But can we reduce the vagueness of ordinary language by using ordinary language?

Goodman: Yes, I think so. For example in *Languages of Art,* the problem of representation is examined. We notice first that "representation" has a dozen or more different uses. A congressman represents a district, a book represents a lot of work, an agent represents a house to be in sound condition, and so on. But we are not dealing with all of these, only with *pictorial* representation or *depiction;* and we try to analyze that notion. We reform ordinary language in this way, after using the same terms but restricting them so that we have something more like a system.

Boenders: Having been told that your philosophy was highly technical, as of course it is in a sense, I was struck by finding *Languages of Art* not very difficult to read. To me it made sense. You used ordinary language. There wasn't much formalism in it. When you were described to me as a kind of formalist, was that untrue?

Goodman: My first book, *The Structure of Appearance,* is surely formalistic; it has a number of different calculi developed in it. On the other hand, the kind of logical precision, the kind of connexity, the kind of systematization that counts, doesn't depend on use of any particular technique. And I am interested to hear you say that you didn't find *Languages of Art* difficult to read, because the chapter on notation in the middle of the book is difficult even though there isn't a single symbol from mathematical logic or anything of the sort in it. Precision is sought rather in the technical use of terms from ordinary language.

Boenders: I was reading again, together with your book, parts of Wittgenstein's *Philosophische Untersuchungen,* where he also reflects on what is perception, what is seeing. Could you tell us how far apart you stand from that kind of unsystematic philosophizing about perception and seeing?

Goodman: I think that your question, in using the term "unsystematic", already points to an important difference. I find Wittgenstein exciting, original, and suggestive; but he treats a topic as a cat does a mouse, teasing it, leaving it, pouncing again. My own efforts are more of the bulldog sort. I try to follow through with certain insights, with certain techniques, and make systematic connections. I once said that science is systematization, and philosophy for me involves organization. Wittgenstein looks at philosophy as spot therapy for particular confusions and says he can stop whenever he wants to—although of course he never wants to. I do philosophy because I can't stop.

Gosselin: Could you perhaps explain to us how the idea came about of stressing the affinities between science and art?

Goodman: Yes, I can do that within the next two hours, I think! The answer has to be partly historical, biographical, and partly something else. All my life has been lived in the arts and in philosophy, but it was only very late in 1968, that I ever wrote anything combining the two. I had become increasingly aware that the revelation we get from science (I am talking about theoretical science) and the revelation we get from art are very much alike. When a scientist first relates heat to motion, or the tides to the moon, our world-views are drastically altered. And when we leave an exhibit of the works of an important painter, the world we step into is not the one we left when we went in; we see everything in terms of those works. That illumination from science and illumination from art are thus akin has been obscured only by the absurd misconception of art as mere entertainment.

Boenders: Now are you thinking only of what Kuhn would call revolutionary science, that really deals with something new and comes to major new insights?

Goodman: No, I am talking of science that contributes some new insights, some new understanding; it needn't be totally revolutionary like those of Newton or Einstein. Pictures and music that are not revolutionary may have qualities enabling us to see or hear somewhat differently, discern differences, and make connections that we couldn't make before—to see things in terms of new patterns, visual or auditory. An example of that was a program I worked on at one time where a photographer showed several different shots of the same subjects. He wanted to choose the pictures for a book. He would put several of them on a screen and leave them there for a few minutes, and at first you couldn't see any difference between them. Then he would start talking about the features that he was considering, not so much about what choice to make but what features entered into consideration. And when he got through talking, you had four or five different photographs where you only had one before. Now, that sort of thing is not unrelated to the kind of insight that you get from a scientific advance.

Boenders: You have been working in the field of art yourself, because you have been producing for this very television station a work of art, a multimedia piece. Could you tell us about how you conceived of the project—I mean, in relation to your profession as a philosopher?

Goodman: Yes, in another two hours! Very briefly, I came upon a whole collection of Katharine Sturgis' action drawings of hockey, made from the television screen and for no reason other than the artist's interest in this action. As I looked at them I saw in them as much choreography as calligraphy. So I had the idea of organizing them into sequences, writing a script, gathering a dance company, commissioning an electronic score, and putting all these things together. The idea was to create a novel and worthwhile work of art making use of the ways vision and hearing and all other aspects of experience interact. After you see this production I think you will never again see hockey or the drawings or dance in the same way as before. And many people, including children, who might resist going to a modern dance or an exhibit of drawings, along with other people who would not condescend to go to a hockey game, have found themselves excited and enlightened by this experience.

Boenders: A sort of—application of a discourse on seeing?

Goodman: Of course the work was not developed just as an illustration of theses. But it does serve as such an illustration. It also, I hope, helps rub out the hard line between the elite and the popular. This production has been enthusiastically received by people who are highly versed in avant-garde art as well as by schoolchildren who are hockey worshipers.

Boenders: Having heard that you were doing this kind of thing, I was somewhat surprised when reading *Languages of Art* that you seem not to be working on the basis of concrete works of art, for example, when you are discussing realism. I found these chapters on realism very illuminating for me. Yet, you are not discussing realistic or realist painters.

Goodman: Well, I often cite particular artists and works to illustrate points, but I do not discuss them at length as a critic would. I am not trying to replace the critic or furnish him with criteria for the evaluation of works.

Boenders: But suppose for a moment that a critic takes up some of your insights in writing criticism on particular and concrete works of art, would you like that kind of use?

Goodman: Of course. One novelty in my philosophy of art is recognition of the important role of exemplification. Now, what is exemplification? Well, when you go to find material to cover your sofa or to have a suit made, and you are shown a little swatch of cloth, that swatch is a sample of certain properties and not of others. To make this point clear I have in one of my books a little story of a lady who picks out a sample, a two-by-three-inch sample of cloth, and orders enough to cover a sofa. She says she wants the material for the sofa to be exactly like the sample. What she gets when she opens the bundle is several hundred little pieces two-by-three inches. This illustrates that being a sample or exemplifying is a kind of referential, symbolic relationship obtaining between something that may be as commonplace as a tailor's swatch and certain properties but not others. One of the major ways some works of art function is by such exemplification. And some critics have lately begun to agree with me on this and make use of this notion in their writing.

Gosselin: You do not want to discuss works of art in particular, but in general; still, you treated the question of realism, and I would like to ask you a more precise question about it. Would I be right in saying that a work of art is more realistic as it conveys more information? Take perspective, for instance. If a work of art is in standard perspective, I think it gives us (though perhaps you won't agree) more information than when it is not in such perspective. What do you think about that?

Goodman: At last we have a question that I needn't take two hours to answer. The answer is: *No.* And I think I can give you a convincing illustration of that. Suppose we draw a picture not according to the rules of standard perspective, but the absolute opposite of these so that parallels converge toward us. Now this picture gives exactly the same information as the other. All we have to do is know the clue to reading it. We have to know that in any case. So if we can have a completely different system giving the same information, then it is clear that realism is not a matter of the quantity of information. Perhaps realism amounts more nearly to how easily this information is absorbed as a result of our habits and the way we have been conditioned to one system or another. And I think, in an Oriental community where Western art hadn't invaded, that the more realistic picture would be the one in terms of an oriental perspective and not in terms of a Western one. But "realism" has other uses, too.

Boenders: You often talk about the question of understanding pictures or understanding art. Do you think that your philosophy of art can contribute to understanding art, when we see it or read it or hear it?

Goodman: Yes, I think that a conceptual apparatus that makes sense and is reasonably comprehensive can help. Noticing the importance of exemplification, for instance, and thus realizing that abstract works, though nonrepresentational, are nevertheless referential—that although they don't depict they do stand for certain properties they exemplify—can aid in our grasping of art. But this alone cannot do much in getting a particular person to see what is in a particular picture. That takes experience with the picture and with related pictures and other things. I am not offering what I have written as a way of teaching art appreciation.

Boenders: As a philosopher of science and language, would you say that styles in art are forms of language the artist uses?

Goodman: In *Ways of Worldmaking* there is one chapter called "The Status of Style." When we speak of style, we speak of certain ways of classifying works of art. Style classifications may be very broad, for example, Western style, or very specific, say sixteenth-century Flemish style, or the early style of Corot. These ways of classifying works cut across classifications according to subject, according to medium, and so forth. And when we become sufficiently sensitive to certain works of art, we begin to develop a new sensitivity, we can see something new. This can be very striking; you see a few pictures by a given artist, and the next picture you see by him, you say, "That looks a little like so and so." You are beginning to grasp a new concept that cuts across the old ones. This, I think, underlines what I was saying about the relationship between art and science, for that's what you do in science, too. You begin to see new connections and make new discriminations, and style is a very good example of this.

Boenders: So styles can be very important, in altering our perception of the concrete work of art?

Goodman: Certainly, because perceiving style is perceiving several relationships between a work of art and certain other works of art and other experiences.

Gosselin: Is it a matter of habit?

Goodman: Practice plays a prominent role, along with alert and intelligent looking. Also, of course, habit often stands as something we have to break away from. We tend to hold to an established classification of styles until our attention is somehow called to interesting affinities between works we had pigeonholed under different styles.

Gosselin: Yes, and experience plays a great part in it. The same goes, I think, for the question of the fake, which you have discussed in *Languages of Art.*

Goodman: Yes. We ask ourselves in the case of the Van Meegeren fakes, how is it that no expert could detect them at first, and now almost anybody can? That is because we have certain precedence-classes established for use. If I show you six fakes and six Vermeers, then you are in a pretty good position to tell whether the next one is a fake or not—at least you are a lot better off. But without some such background, you may be at a loss.

Gosselin: But if someone asks you: "Is it important whether this painting is a Van Meegeren or a Vermeer," you would certainly answer yes.

Goodman: Indeed, because development of discrimination and perception of relationships is a fundamental part of the understanding of works of art.

Boenders: Is there a question of truth in art, I mean, can an artist be untrue to himself or false, can he behave falsely in his work?

Goodman: Only metaphorically, I think, or at least not in the primary use of "true". I like to keep the term "true" for statements. Statements in a language are true or they are false. I don't like to speak of a picture as being true or false, since it doesn't literally make a statement. But I would rather say that a picture can be right or wrong the way a design can be right or wrong.

Boenders: But you cannot say that in some sense an artist can be untrue to himself by working in a very loose way, by not doing his very best, living up to his standard?

Goodman: Of course it is perfectly good usage in English to say that an artist is untrue to his aim. But here again, as with "representation," we need to develop a technical language free of the ambiguities of ordinary usage.

Gosselin: You are always very cautious regarding problems of aesthetics.

Goodman: Some think I am too daring.

Boenders: I found very little in your book about appreciation of a work of art, although you write on it at the end of the book.

Goodman: The term "appreciation of art" and the term "beauty" and a few others are nearly taboo for me because they have been associated with so much nonsense. Rather than appreciation of art I am concerned with the understanding of art, the grasping of it.

Boenders: Are you then not using "understanding" also in a metaphorical sense, because normally we speak of appreciating a work of art?

Goodman: Well, "appreciating" seems to me to suggest that art is purely entertainment, enjoyment, emotion. The habit of thinking of science as purely intellectual and art as purely emotional has muddled much thinking about both art and science.

Boenders: I agree with you. I think that's one of the basic insights in your book. When I stand in front of a Mondrian, it's useless to say: Well, I am moved. We must indeed understand the picture first of all. But that is not true of all art, I think. Let's give a very crude example of one of the late String Quartets by Beethoven. Is it a question of understanding? Isn't plain emotion what matters here?

Goodman: You mean just listening to it without understanding it? Understanding, for me, means grasping its forms, its patterns, its relationships. Do you mean that just bathing in the music is the important thing?

Boenders: I would say you must bathe in some works of art before you understand them.

Goodman: The two things can alternate historically. Initial excitement about a work may lead me to examine it further and understand it better, and that better understanding and the process of achieving it may give a new and greater satisfaction. But this goes for science too. If there were no excitement, no thrill, no satisfaction, science would stagnate. Emotion enters into both art and science, but it is no more the sole end in the one than the other.

Boenders: I agree with you. Reading *Languages of Art*, once again I was thrilled by some of the insights and some of the very detailed reasoning. Yet, at the end I was asking myself, are the results commensurate with all these brilliant insights? This is a very straightforward criticism. How do you feel about it when I put it this way?

Goodman: Languages of Art, because it is somewhat revolutionary, has aroused a good deal of controversy. On the one hand, the *Journal of Aesthetics and Art Criticism*, in the foreword to a recent symposium on the book, calls it a book destined to influence aesthetic thinking to a degree far beyond the expectations of the aestheticians of the time of its publication, and Howard Gardner writes that the book almost singlehandedly converted the dreary field of the philosophy of art into a major and vigorous study. On the other hand, some critics, as you remarked earlier this afternoon, think that the book leaves aesthetics just where it was. Perhaps it does, in much the way the automobile left the horse and buggy where it was and aviation leaves the railroad where it was.

Gosselin: That is your pluralism?

Goodman: Not so much my pluralism as an aversion to much that passed as philosophy of art before. One way my book leaves philosophy of art where it was is in bypassing some of the problems that traditional philosophy of art thought were the most important, such as the nature and standards of beauty. It reformulates some problems and questions, and deals with some different ones. You won't find in my book treatises on the sublime, or rhapsodies on appreciation and creativity. In this way, it does leave aesthetics where it was.

Boenders: That is, you don't conceive such problems as your task?

Goodman: Obviously one of the questions, and certainly a legitimate question, in any treatise that touches on these matters is "What is art?" But in one of my chapters I suggest that the more fundamental question is "When is art?" and that "What is art?" is secondary to that. And one of the delights in working on this was to find that by looking at it in this way we can deal with the case of the found object and the case of conceptual art. Here are objects or events which are not works of art but which may function as such. On the other hand, works of art do not always function as such; for example, if we use a Rembrandt painting to patch up a door. And it is in terms of the function, I think, that we have to understand what art is.

Gosselin: That's where your symptoms of the aesthetic come in. You have spoken about symptoms, not about criteria for knowing what is a work of art, but of symptoms of the aesthetic.

Goodman: This is not altogether a matter of policy, but the result of facing a very difficult problem of definition and construction. Consider what we do when we ask a question like "What is a work of art?" or "What is a fish?" We have to start from ordinary practice and then we try to fit a formula to the practice. We may here revise the formula or revise the practice or both. We revise the practice when for systematic reasons we decide that after all a whale is not a fish. And eventually, if we are going to answer the question "What is art?" we will have to arrive at a satisfactory formula. Until then, symptoms are the best I can do.

Boenders: Rather than the definition, the question the public asks itself on entering an exhibition hall is "When is art?" When is art the case in this object? For instance when the artist says that it is art, or when the critic says that it is art? What is the criterion for something to be art?

Goodman: That question I have answered only to the extent, as I have said, of giving certain symptoms of the way a work of art functions as a symbol. If its functioning exhibits all these symptoms, then very likely the object is a work of art. If it shows almost none, then it probably isn't.

Gosselin: Of course the problem for the art gallery director and for the museum director and the collector is to choose works of art.

Goodman: That's true. But we have to bear in mind that we must distinguish very sharply—as many people have not—between the question "What is art?" and the question "What is good art?" Now, the symptoms I have suggested are symptoms of functioning as a work of art, not of functioning as a *good* work of art. And if we start defining "what is a work of art" in terms of what is good art, I think we are hopelessly confused. For unfortunately, most works of art are bad.

Boenders: We haven't tackled technical problems, but I had prepared a question regarding a technicality. I think you have proved here and now, that you can be a technical philosopher and at the same time someone who can really talk in understandable language. But I want to ask an earlier question in a somewhat different form: When a technical philosopher uses a formalistic language, such as mathematical logic, is it for you important that at least it should be translatable, and that if he should be asked to he can give the translation?

Goodman: I think it is very important. Not only should the formula be translatable but also derived from an actual practice. It has to be refined and developed if we are going to have a vocabulary in terms of which we can capture subtle distinctions and relationships and concepts that cut across the traditional ones. A somewhat related question often is asked, "Does this sort of work do anything about solving the problems of the present-day world?" And the answer to that, I think, is the question: What do you think are the problems of the present-day world? If you mean poverty, war—

Boenders: Then you had better become a politician.

Goodman: Exactly. That is not philosophy's primary business. And what has contributed enormously to current misunderstanding of the nature of art and science alike is the idea that they must be justified in terms of practical results. This, I think, mistakes ends for means and means for ends. Social betterment and technological progress are not the goals of Shakespeare's works or Einstein's but may help make possible such works and our increased understanding through them. The overriding effort is toward removing confusions, discerning distinctions and connections, perceiving more sensitively and fully, gaining new insights—in short, toward advancement of the understanding.

Sources and Acknowledgments

Permissions by the editors or publishers of material previously published are gratefully acknowledged. The initial appearances of such material are listed below, along with locus of use in this book. Extractions, additions, and other revisions since first publication are frequent.

SOURCE:	USED IN:
Journal of Aesthetics and Art Criticism	
39 (1981) 273–289	I,2&5; III,4&5; IV,5&6
40 (1982) 281–283	IV,9
Art Education 36 (1983) 34–41	V,1
Arts Spectrum (Harvard) 2 (1975) 4	V,3
Cognition 12 (1982) 212–217	I,6
Communication & Cognition 13 (1980) 169–172	I,1
Critical Inquiry	
6 (1979) 125–130	III,2
7 (1980) 103–119	IV,1
7 (1981) 799–801	IV,2
8 (1981) 121–132	III,1
Erkenntnis	
12 (1978) 153–179	I,2&3; III,3-6
12 (1978) 281–291	II,3
Leonardo 4 (1971) 359–360	I,3
Midwest Studies in Philosophy 2 (1977) 212–213	II,4
The Monist 58 (1974) 339–342	I,4

The New Criterion 2 (1983–84) 9–14	V,5
New Literary History 14 (1982–83) 269–272	IV,4
Journal of Philosophy	
70 (1973) 166	IV,7
74 (1977) 317–338	III,7
Philosophy and Literature 6 (1982) 162–164	IV,3
Ratio 20 (1978) 49–51	IV,8
Synthèse 45 (1980) 211–215	II,2

Basic Abilities Required for Understanding and Creation in the Arts, Nelson Goodman et al. (Final Report Project No. 9-0283; Washington, D.C.: U.S. Department of Health, Education, and Welfare, Office of Education, 1972)	V,2
Language and Ontology, W. Leinfellner, E. Kraemer, J. Schank, eds. (Vienna: Holder-Pichler-Tempsky, 1982) 31–38	II,1
What Is Dance?, Roger Copeland and Marshall Cohen, eds. (New York: Oxford University Press, 1983) 80–85	III,1
Past, Present, East and West, Sherman Lee (New York: George Braziller, 1983) 17–18	V,4

Name Index

Subject Index

Abilities, 151, 156–158, 164
About, 99–107, 133
Absolutely about, 101
Absolutism, 46–47
Abstract art. See Nonrepresentational art
Acceptability, ultimate, 38, 40
Aesthetic, 5–9, 84–85, 92, 133–134, 138;
  symptoms of, 135–138, 198–199
Aesthetics, 19, 146–158, 192–200
Allegory, 130
Allographic, 139–140, 144
Allusion, 65–66
Ambiguity, 17, 18, 56, 59, 72, 73, 111,
  124, 196
Analog, 16, 17
Analytic/synthetic distinction, 94–95, 190
Antinomies, Kantian, 32
Apparatus, general, 44–45
Application. See Denotation
Appreciation, 153, 196–197, 198
Art, 2, 5–9, 19, 69–71, 80–86, 109–145,
  146–188, 192–199
Articulate, 18, 86
Attenuation, 136
Audience, 5, 150, 158–162, 181
Autographic, 139–140, 144

Belief, 40, 90, 127–128
Biography, 126
Brain, 14–19, 149

Catastrophism, 21
Categories. See Kinds
Categorization, 7, 37–38
Chains, referential, 39, 44, 62–69, 70, 124,
  137

Class, 29, 36, 49–50, 51
Classes, calculus of. See Set theory
Classification of works, 195
Cognition, 7–9, 14–28, 35, 84–85,
  146–150, 150–158, 164–167, 172–173,
  178–180
Coherence, 37
Compound terms, 60, 64–65, 75, 76, 78,
  79
Comprehension. See Understanding
Concepts, basic, 163–164
Conflict, 29–34, 39
Consolidation, 100
Construction, 34–37, 44–48, 50–53,
  198–199
Containment, 58
Content, 43–44
Context, 25, 33, 87, 93, 98–99, 134
Convention, 43–44, 67–69, 81, 112, 116,
  127–128
Correspondence, 37, 39, 49
Creativity, 154, 198
Credibility, permanent. See Acceptability,
  ultimate
Criticism, 82–83, 84, 166, 193

Dance, 159
Dance notation, 56
Deceptiveness, 9
Definition, constructional, 44–48, 50–53,
  198–199
Denotation, 25, 48–50, 55–63, 69–70,
  71–75, 80–81, 83, 86, 87–94, 96–99,
  132, 135
Denotational level, 62–66, 68, 136–137
Density, 18, 57–58, 86, 136–137

exemplify. — the literal
expression — the metaphorical